T0115045

GETTING OLD

SUCKS IF YOU LET IT!

A SPECIAL MESSAGE TO MY DAUGHTERS

A HUMOROUS GUIDE TO LIFE OLD
CHALLENGES OF AGING

BARBARA LEIGH HARTENFELD

BALBOA
PRESS

A DIVISION OF HAY HOUSE

Balboa Press books may be ordered through booksellers or by contacting:

Balboa Press
A Division of Hay House
1663 Liberty Drive
Bloomington, IN 47403
www.balboapress.com
1 (877) 407-4847

Printed in the United States of America.

ISBN: 978-1-4525-8482-9 (sc)
ISBN: 978-1-4525-8484-3 (hc)
ISBN: 978-1-4525-8483-6 (e)

Library of Congress Control Number: 2013918502

Balboa Press rev. date: 11/14/2013

Table of Contents

This book is lovingly dedicated to my daughters, Tracy and Tricia, to my sisters and to all the women in my life that have made a difference in mine. To my mother, I wish you could have been here.

Life's Clock

The clock of life is wound but once
And no man has the power,
To tell just where the hand will stop
At late or early hour.

Now is the only time we own
Live...love life with a will.

Place no faith in tomorrow,
For the Clock may then be still

Author Unknown

Preface

I have heard before that you begin aging the minute you are born. Pretty depressing don't you think? Aging definitely has it's mysteries but it also has a lot of fun surprises-little unexpected twists and turns-that happen when you least expect them and that is what makes this journey we call "Life" so interesting. There hopefully are a lot of years between birth and the end of life, so my dear daughters and friends, I ask that you enjoy the journey. Enjoy *my* journey as I share the wisdom and sense of humor I have been forced to develop in spite of Mother Nature's attempt to try my patience every chance she gets. You will find that we women are all sisters on this trip and the bigger the army, the less painful the battle!

I started this book because my daughters tired of my advice on aging and told me to write a book instead. I gave them the short version as a Christmas gift several years ago and have been adding to it since then, realizing my story could be of some use to all women. After all, we may have different skin color, speak in different languages, live in different parts of the world, practice different religions, but bottom line is, we are all Women. We address aging issues and how they affect our lives in different ways.

In my particular journey, there are *so* many things my mother didn't tell me! As a result, growing older has at times been an agonizing adventure so I would like to share some common sense secrets to make your journey more fun. I have injected humor in most circumstances. After all, if you can't laugh at yourself, who else can and get away with it?

No matter what your age, we all live in incredible times. It is up to us to become aware of and appreciate those times and to study the history of the generations that came before us. It is also our duty to pass on our own history to our daughters and granddaughters not only to make their journeys a bit less painful, but to let them realize that no matter when or where we live on this earth, we are real women who live, love, laugh and cry. We have hopes, dreams and ambitions. We are different but we are also a lot alike and we all have stories to share.

This is my story.

Introduction

In my particular journey, there are *so* many things my mother didn't tell me! As a result, growing older has at times been an agonizing adventure. Since my mother died at the age of 68, when I was in my mid-forties, she hasn't been around for me to ask my many questions about the mysteries of life as a woman. Before she passed, I thought I knew *everything*, so I didn't ask her. As I plan on outliving her, I am sure there will be numerous events in my life to come that I will have to struggle through in her absence. In this book I have tried to share all my joys of aging as well as my aches, pains, physical dilemmas and emotional side effects with my daughters as I encounter them so they aren't as blindsided as I have been. They still don't know that my experiences could actually save them a lot of headache and heartache because right now, like me, they think they know everything-always have, most likely always will! I *could* be really mean and not share anything with them but perhaps I am a sadist at heart and continue, much to their anguish, explaining in gruesome detail, my own aging process. They appreciate *this* about as much as my idea of having my ashes after my death; put into lockets so they could wear "me" around their necks!

I have also included a few of my more extraordinarily embarrassing experiences my daughters don't know about and am certain don't really want to hear. But, as I said, they know *so much more* than I, so I can't resist any opportunity to gross them out!

It has taken me ten years to write this book. I have often felt it would never get finished but then my life isn't finished yet so perhaps that is why the book isn't finished yet either. Each additional year brings more evolutionary surprises and I believe destiny has decided I needed the opportunity to share as much as possible to make this book as complete as possible. Not that it will change their lives, but at least I will know that I have tried my very best to help my daughters and other young women avoid many of the same misconceptions and mistakes I have made and make all of you realize that like myself, you may not know as much as you think you do. It won't hurt to listen!

I begin my journey as a teenager-after all, isn't that when the aging process really begins? From infancy to that time, does anyone ever think about "aging"? No. We just grow, are taken care of, decisions made for us and basically enjoy life. Nothing too complicated. We wake up in the morning, eat a breakfast that we don't have to prepare ourselves, brush our teeth, get dressed and go out and play. Then there is lunch, more play, maybe a nap and dinner time, bath time, prayers, good-night hugs from mom and dad and then we get up and start all over again. How truly tranquil. That is until Puberty. That's when it all starts getting complicated.

Near as I can tell, that's when I felt my first "growing pains". It is not easy being a teenager. After surviving two teenage daughters myself, I can realize now that it wasn't any easier for my parents. This was the time I thought cheerleading, talking on the phone, who was going to take me to the Prom and along with my changing body, a fascination with the mysteries of sex were among the top ten on my priority list of wonders and "what ifs". I didn't want to seem childish so I never asked my mom any questions about any of these certain I could figure it out better on my own. Heaven knows sex was the *last* subject my mother wanted to talk to me about anyway! She still dressed in a closet-that's why all the older homes had big walk-in closets, don't you know! I have my doubts my father ever saw her naked in daylight! I was programmed to get embarrassed hearing my mother and her girlfriends talk about "periods" in a whisper on their card club nights. The word "menstruation" or "the curse" was never discussed in the presence of a man. Until our new generation, the baby boomers who began having father's present at child birth, "that time of the month", cramps, swollen breasts, backache and swelling related to menstruation, and sanitary belts, (do you even know what I'm talking about?), were not topics of discussion for mixed company. My mother's generation never let go of that behavior and they wanted us to have the same proprieties.

This is how I was raised-a child of the sixties-and I had one heck of a time breaking those patterns. I remember waiting in my country doctor's office shortly before the birth of my first daughter and a woman about my mother's age, noticing my immense bulk asked me, "And when are you going to get *sick?*" *Sick?* I didn't know I was going to get "sick" on top of all the labor pains, water-breaking, bleeding, and having a 12 centimeter head come out of 10 centimeter cavity! And now I had to look forward to throwing up and diarrhea too? Oh! I was so naïve! That proves my point that my mother should have educated me a teensy bit more about sex and having babies. And that wasn't all! Read on.

Eavesdropper that I was, my father and his friends had a *great* time talking about women's "problems" and joking behind their wives backs! My father *swore* that my mother went through *"the change"* for 20 years. (Good Grief! She was raising five children!). Every time my mother cried, or lost her temper or threw a pan into the wall, dad would blame it *on "the change"*. When my little sister cut her long blonde ringlets at the root and said, "Well, the scissors were just laying there doing nothing!" and my mother lost it, dad would blame it on *"the change"*. When my older brother and our cousin burned down the field across the street and my mother lost it, dad would blame it on *"the change"*. When my younger brother got his penis caught in his zipper and my mother lost it, dad would blame it on *"the change"*. If there wasn't enough room in the refrigerator for dad's beer and he took out good food and put it on the counter to rot so he could have "a cold one" any time he wanted and my mother lost it, he blamed it on *"the change"*. When we all moved into a house that wasn't finished yet and dad dropped a hammer on mom's head through the second floor floorboards and my mother lost it, he blamed it on *"the change"*. You see, while women were raised to keep female conditions private, men were taught they were allowed to make them the butt of their jokes. Ahhh, life in the male-dominated sixties!

I wish I had some of my father's stories to pass around on the internet now and Pre Menstrual Syndrome, (PMS) still hadn't been coined yet! They would have had a ball with *that* one!

My mother was from a transitional stage of her own. While she was growing up with a "subservient stage" mother, she was forced by the Big One-WW II—to become the first generation of women on a whole, to work in factories on assembly lines, raise children on their own, smoke publicly, (instead of behind the outhouse), form all-women sports teams due to absentee men who were away fighting the war. Little did men anticipate that when they returned from the war that women would like their new responsibilities and interests associated with their new roles and really wouldn't *want* to go back home and to be *their husbands' mothers!*

Hartenfeld Family Album. Photographer, Rolland Hartenfeld—deceased circa 1949

A little more about that era, the Transitional Stage. Women went from "subservient, stay-at-home and raise the children" stage to "It's okay if you want to work outside the home as long as you have dinner on the table for me at six o'clock" (John Wayne) stage. Here are more nuances from this stage for your curiosity and enlightenment:

Eisenhower was in the White House. Tupperware parties were invented and everyone you knew had the same brown clock they got as a hostess gift on their living room wall next to a mirrored shadow box. Three-bedroom tract homes were filling the country side. Women, and their little girls wore white gloves and white shoes, (only after Easter and before Labor Day) and no one was afraid to justify "In God We Trust". Men did "men's work" and women did "women's work" and no one ever thought of crossing the line. Men would never be caught dead doing the dishes, vacuuming the floors or changing a diaper.

Mothers didn't have to talk to their daughters about sex. They had a little book called *"Growing Up and Liking It"* with pictures of ovaries and fallopian tubes which my mother gave me and told me, "Go to your bedroom and read it." Before she closed my bedroom door, she said, "If you have any questions when you are done, let me know". Then I'm sure she desperately prayed, "Please God, don't let her have any questions!" I am also sure she sat at the kitchen table with her coffee and a pack of cigarettes "losing it" as she waited for me to come downstairs. Hard to believe I was her *second* daughter! Do you suppose her panic had something to do with *"the change"*!

Never much for reading, I mostly looked at the pictures and flashed through the book hurriedly looking for a picture of a penis but found none. I later realized that this wasn't really a book about sex, but a promotion published by Kotex for sanitary napkins and belts. Pictures of the big purple or blue box and a tiny box that contained the sanitary belt that looked more like a hook-and-line, were all over the place! The one thing I most definitely remember with animosity about those is how it hurt to wear a sanitary belt while wearing a girdle, (tight elastic thing that had hooks inside to hold up your nylon stockings before panty hose were invented), to hold up my black-seamed nylon hose, at the same time and having the belt hook bite into my behind if I sat down wrong. This is indeed where the phrase "Bite me" started! (Girls, thank the period gods that you don't have any idea what I am talking about!)

"Growing Up and Liking It" didn't tell me anything about *that* either! It also didn't tell me that boys would sit in the top row of the bleachers watching the cheerleaders, (me), do cartwheels to see who was "on the rag". You see, the boys of the sixties still had the same sense of humor and sense of morality and respect as their fathers.

"Do you have any questions?" mom timidly asked as I came out of my room.

"Nope" I said, and left the house to play touch football with the neighbor boys. Boy, I'll bet she was relieved! Only one more daughter to go and her motherly obligation of explaining sex, puberty and the facts of life was done!

I *did* notice that the older I got, the more the boys liked to tackle me at touch football and the longer they kept me on the ground after the tackle. *"Growing Up and Liking It"* didn't tell me anything about *that* either! I just know I liked it and I wondered if the boys knew more than I did about sex. I could have cared less about sex before I hit puberty. After all, the only penis I ever saw was my little brother's when

I changed his pants and that wasn't anything to get excited about. I *still* didn't know how to "do it!" My first thoughts were that men and women had sex from the penis to the breast since those were parts of the anatomy men seem to talk about most in jokes that I wasn't supposed to be hearing until I was in 7th grade. Come to think of it, I did actually have a "sex talk" with my dad once about the sign that hung in his grocery store that said:

"Old Golfers Never Die...they just lose their balls!"

When I asked my dad what that meant, he just said, "You'll understand when you get older!" Or... "go ask your mother!" That was it-my father's one and only contribution!

As curious as I was about sex, I was scared to death of it because my father swore that if I ever came home pregnant I wouldn't have a home anymore. *Lordie!* I didn't know how to have sex, but I sure didn't want to lose my home! That stymied my curiosity for a while.

Like most other girls in a protective environment like mine, I worried about being pregnant if I "petted" in a parked car and got all excited. *Fat chance of that!* When I started dating, my father installed four high-beam spot lights across the front porch and turned them on the minute my date and I pulled into the driveway. As quickly as I could, I would run from my boyfriend-du-jour's car to the front door and dad would still be there at the top of stairs glaring at me. "Do you have anything you want to tell me?"

About the very closest discussion I ever had with my mother about sex was at Christmas one year when I was about 17 years old. My sister and I were helping her put the Christmas tree up. Mom was holding the tree steady and my sister and I were screwing the bolts of the tree stand into the trunk. When mom felt the tree was finally straight, she told us girls, *"Okay, everybody screw!"*

The tree dropped to the floor when my sister and I rolled over laughing hysterically after hearing those words come out of our mother's mouth! When mom finally "caught on", (she was *so* naïve!), she blushed, threw her arms up in the air and told us how disgusting we were as she retreated to her bedroom!

Come to think about it, *sex* was the *last thing* I wanted to talk about with my mother anyway! Before my wedding at nearly twenty-one years old, she was still telling me about "the seed theory". God planted it and you had a baby. *Good grief, mom!* I think she knew I was getting married but the thought of me actually having sex was out of her realm of reality.

Now you have to remember that I am a baby boomer-a member of another "transitional stage" of the 20th century woman—the bra burners; first round of "super moms", first generation to take *the Pill* rather than produce the expected 4.8 children; first woman in my family to get a college degree and actually have an independent career *and* a family; and first generation of young women who think losing your virginity *before* marriage is an advantage and the first step toward a healthy attitude toward sex…according to the Kinsey Report and Helen Gurley Brown.

"You wouldn't try on a pair of shoes before you bought them, would you?" was one of my favorite sayings, yet I was a virgin until the ripe old age of twenty when I got married. It wasn't because I was so virtuous-it was because I was scared to death of my father!

As I got older, I realized that mom (and dad), didn't tell me about a lot of other things too. These are the things I *wish* my mother would have told me:

1. When did you *really* start feeling like a "grown-up"?
2. Did you have morning sickness or gain a lot of weight when you were pregnant?
3. When did your hair start turning gray?

4. When did you get your first wrinkles and what should I do when I get them?

5. Why don't your pants suddenly fit you in the crotch anymore when you hit 35?

6. When did you find that first rogue hair on your chin, your breasts, your nose, or in your ears?

7. When did those hairs turn gray and your eyes get so bad that you couldn't "see" them anymore to pluck them?

8. Why did you need false teeth at the age of forty? Will I?

9. When did you start feeling the pain of arthritis?

10. When did you start menopause? *Really!* Not like my dad said! I can't believe it would really last for *twenty years!* How long did it really last?

11. Did menopause make you gain weight?

12. How old were you when you quit shaving your legs? Your armpits?

13. When did you first notice you may need a hearing aid?

14. How did you keep your heart from breaking every time one of your children got *their* hearts broken?

Scientists say aging is hereditary and that all you have to do to see yourself in the future is to look at your mother. Now, I would also have to agree that environment and lifestyle, (nature vs. nurture), has a lot to do with it, but generally the biggest contributors are in the preverbal gene pool.

Big piece of advice here for you guys out there, too: Before making a commitment, when you are looking for a life partner-look at her mother! Ask yourself, does mom greet you at the door in sweats with chocolate stains and baby barf on them, and smelly hair pulled up in a knot, or does she look like she just came home from the office, the gym or the beauty parlor? Or maybe she doesn't greet you at the door! Does she "grunt" when you walk in front of the television or does she look like she's going to throw a knitting needle at you from across the room when you walk in the front door? Does mom smoke or is that why she doesn't have any wrinkles on her face? Does she shave her legs, (and ugh, her armpits), on a regular basis? Does mom go to the gym and eat healthy foods? Take a good long look at her mother boys! Your wife may turn into her in twenty years! Yep! Most likely!

Same thing for you girls! Look at the daddies! Even if your boyfriend looks super hot now shooting hoops with the guys in his sexy, loosie-goosie shorts, no shirt and sweat running down his chest and his six-pack that spells out, "I'm hot"—stop and think! If he loves his beer before, during and after the game, and then gobbles down a super sized burger and fries … or two … or three-his metabolism is in its peak right now, *but look at daddy*. Does daddy have a beer belly that looks like it might "pop" when he bends over to grab a potato chip off the coffee table on his way to the remote? When you run your fingers through his hair, do you come out with stragglers? *Look at daddy!* Don't let silly little things like "love at first sight" and so-called animal magnetism cloud your thinking. Your husband may turn into his dad in twenty years too! Ask yourself, "Is this really my soul mate"? Look at mommy and daddy and really think about it! Okay, enough advice for now.

This is what this book is all about. This is for you, my dear daughters and for any woman who doesn't like surprises. I am sharing my life's journey with you and telling you exactly what I have experienced. You can learn from it and make your life better or at the least, just not be as surprised as I was when these inevitable life changes come into your life-and believe me *they will!*

I have dedicated a portion of this book to what was happening in the world around me and my own personal family history for your enjoyment certainly, but mostly to encourage everyone to experience the joys I have by being aware of the world around you and seeing how much it affects your life and by researching your family tree to discover all the names in the family Bible were *real people* with lives, challenges and dreams of their own. You don't really know who you are until you know where you came from.

I always told my daughters I would write a book about getting older someday. They laughed at me and said, "Yeah, yeah, and yeah!" Well, here it is! I want your undivided attention!

(Like THAT'S possible!)

CHAPTER ONE

Ahh... Gentle Youth!

Barbara and Bonnie
Hartenfeld Family Album. Photographer, Donald
Hartenfeld—deceased circa 1948

Aging never enters a youthful mind. It is just something your parents and grandparents do.

I was a happy child. I didn't have a care in the world. Of course none of this may interest any of you young women today, but I had my cousins to play kick ball and baseball with in the alley and they shared their toy guns and cowboy hats with me. I always got to be Annie Oakley because my sister was busy inside playing with dolls.

I spent every weekend I could at my grandma's house taking walks, playing croquet, and skipping stones on the lake. My grandma taught me how to clean house, sew and crochet. My grandpa taught me how to ice fish in a shanty on the lake and clean a fish. There were lots of cousins at picnics with baloney sandwiches, Kool-Aid, potato chips and sweet pickles. We all raked leaves into a pile, avoided the dog poop as we played in them, relished the fall aroma in the air while grandpa burned the leaves across the street in the field. Yep! You could burn leaves, without a permit, anywhere you darn well wanted to back then!

On a summer's day, I would fall asleep in a hammock until sprinkles of rain wakened me or my grandma stuck her head out the back door to yell, "Supper is ready!", as she let the screen door slam behind her. My grandpa, knowing I would be there on Friday nights, always left two devils food cookies in his lunch box on the shelf in the garage so I could "discover" them when he got home from work. Even without technology, I was a spoiled child!

My brothers, sisters and I built tents out of sheets and blankets over the clothes line in the back yard and it would take an hour to dress in our snow suits, gloves and boots to build snow forts and snow people until we couldn't feel our toes and fingers anymore. In the summer, I caught fireflies and put them in jars with holes in the tops but they were all dead by morning anyway. I loved *SPAM* brand with the key on top sandwiches and my mother always had plenty on hand. After a big rain storm, my siblings and I plugged the sewer drains with leaves and went swimming in the street. We harvested "buckeyes", (only people from Ohio would understand that one), in the fall when they fell from the trees. We would fill our little red wagon with those brown and tan beauties and my mother or dad would find them soft, green and moldy, months later in the garage or a closet in the house. These were simpler, less complicated times—not a computer, I-pod, or E-phone in sight. Yet I remember being very happy.

Long after my mother passed away, one of her lifelong friends told me that I was always "so damn happy as a kid that I wanted to slap you sometimes!" *Ahhh,* life really was good! And then *Puberty* hit! Here's where it all begins.

My *first real significant sign of aging* of course, was my period when I was 15 years old. "This is when your life really begins!", or so I heard. All of a sudden you are catapulted into womanhood just because you now have all the capabilities of producing children. Until it actually happened, I had to "fake" my periods because all the other girls my age already had theirs and I listened to them complaining about cramps, MIDOL and messy pads and I learned the lingo enough to get away with my deception. I would tell the swim coach, "I can't swim today. *"My period."* And the instructor would mark an X in her book. So I kept track myself-every four weeks, "I can't swim today-my period." When I wasn't swimming and she wasn't looking I would roam the halls until it was time to go back to the pool. I liked swimming, but my hair would look like a jelly fish the rest of the day. One time when I was "faking" my period, I got bored sitting in the pool rafters pretending to do homework, and went into the girls locker room and switched everyone's underwear. I put the D+ bra of the *not-so-skinny girl's* into a training bra locker and threw a black silk half-slip into the rafters. After I went unnoticed back into the pool area and the class was dismissed, everyone went running to the locker room to shower and change only to find the slip I had thrown to the rafters smoldering on the overhead lights. *"Guess I didn't see that one coming!"*

You should have heard the screaming as the other girls filed into the locker room, dripping wet and confused. No one had the right underwear! (Small, large or extra-large wonder!)

The gym teacher yelled, *"Hartenfeld! You get in here!* You put back everyone's underwear where they belong!"

"Who, me? *Why, me?"* Now how in the world would I know who fit what underwear? I went onto my next class giggling under my breath.

Of course I didn't know anything about it! I was the perfect student, cute and little, so I got out of that one all together and by now, that swim coach is certainly dead, so who cares? I had to keep up my "good girl image"! And the best part was-no one suspected I hadn't started my period yet. No harm, no foul.

No one that is except my worried mother. But, why on earth would I even *want* one? I would much rather play touch football! I was nearly sixteen years old before "the curse" came! My mother threatened to take me to the doctor to see why I wasn't "maturing normally" because my older sister started her period when she was only nine. She was *sure* there was something wrong with me!! I guess her threat matured me because I started my period not long after that and I didn't have to go to the doctor.

I started my first period at my aunt's house one hot summer day when I was babysitting. Even at fifteen, I still didn't feel elated or anything. My aunt helped me out by giving me a Kotex and one of those god-awful, butt-biting sanitary belts that I read about in that darn book that didn't have a single picture of a penis in it! When I got home, I found out my aunt had already called my mother and told her of the *"blessed event"*. I guess it was the old "My daughter is finally a woman Hot Line!"

The absolute minute I walked in the door, all my mother could say was, "Did Aunt Evelyn show you how to attach the pad to the sanitary belt?" (Did she suspect I hadn't read the book?) She said nothing about this being "the beginning of my womanhood" or how "lucky" I was to have this promise of a child-bearing future. No sympathy. No good advice. No "Okay, you're a woman now, but *Please, don't get pregnant!"*

(That's what I used on my oldest daughter!) All she asked was "Did Aunt Evelyn show you how to attach the pad to the sanitary belt?"

I think my sister was more excited about it than my mother or me. After all, up until that time, she had a freak for a sister! She probably told everyone she knew that now she was certain I wasn't a boy!

I had awful cramps right from the beginning. I passed out once giving a speech in class because the pain was so bad! The school nurse had to drive me home and she had a long discussion with my mother about what to do about it. Of course, I was sent out of the room so they could have this discussion about me and my menses alone!

I discovered that a hot cup of tea and a MIDOL would help relax me enough to get through the severe cramping each month. One night, in the middle of the night, the cramping was getting unbearable. I went downstairs to make a cup of tea. At sixteen, I must have looked like a little old lady with severe osteoporosis all slouched over, holding my stomach and groaning with every step. I filled the tea kettle, (we didn't have microwave ovens yet), and turned the gas range on. Just then, I had a double-you-over cramp and passed out cold right next to the open flames of the gas range. About that time, my mother came downstairs and found me with my hair only *inches* away from the flames. She screamed as she pulled me away from the fire. Needless to say, *that* woke me up! But the cramps were still there!

After that, my mother always told me to wake her up when I had cramps so I wouldn't burn myself or the house up. I did just that and it warms my heart to remember that she would sit there in the middle of the night with a cup of coffee and her cigarettes while I sipped on my hot tea and she rubbed my back while I laid tummy-down on a heating pad—until the crisis passed. Thank you, mom.

Boy! I never saw my brothers or my dad going through any of this! So unfair! I really *should* have been a boy!

When I was about seventeen, our family doctor decided to put me on birth control pills to help regulate my periods and lesson the cramps. Birth control pills, (A.K.A. "the pill"), were relatively new at that time and I think my country doctor read somewhere in a medical journal that birth control pills would help cramping. I became his guinea pig. I took *"the pill"* but wanted to make sure *no one* knew about it! Being a slut in those days was social suicide! I swore my mother to secrecy-not even my sister needed to know! A lot of good that did. My sister knew right from the start but then I always could count on her to keep a secret! Nothing to worry about.

But, *wait a minute*! This could be a good thing! I would be more sophisticated than the other girls because I was already "on the pill". I could start having sex with anyone who thought knowing a girl on "the pill" was cool, and never get caught. I could join the sexual revolution! One problem though…my dad! He would KILL me if he ever found out! I wouldn't dare let this out. Every guy in my high school would be on me like a dog in heat!

So I kept this big secret to myself until my mother one day told me, "I told Aunt Mary Alice that we had you on 'the pill' and Aunt Mary just snickered."

Oh, My Gawd! My Aunt thinks I'm a Whore…*and my mother has a big mouth!*

HARDWARE

The women of my generation had two choices: sanitary pads or sanitary pads. We didn't have re-adjustable wings, thins, minis, extra longs, extra absorbents, barrier protectors, absorbing pores or scented panty liners. My mother made me swear never to use a tampon! She said

I would lose my virginity if I did. I didn't even know what a "virginity" was! "Only *married* women can wear tampons!" she told me.

Since I was one of the cheerleaders that the dirty little boys watched from the top of bleachers, I decided to borrow a tampon. I didn't want anyone to know that I didn't know how to use them so I didn't ask. So, cardboard and all went up…at least *tried* to go up! To make it worse, I told my girlfriend how hard I flowed during my periods so she said, "Here, try two at a time. Just slide them up next to each other."

I nearly passed out! I already had cramps to beat the band and now I was trying to shove two cardboard containers with parachute strings up inside a never-before-used vagina! It was a struggle but I finally got them in half-way and started perspiring heavily and got *really* dizzy so I leaned my head up against the cool steel toilet paper dispenser to "take a break".

My girlfriend could hear me moaning in the stall, "Are you okay in there?" she asked. "You *did* take the cardboard off didn't you?" "Uh… well of course I did!" I responded. Okay. So you are supposed to take the cardboard off? "I'm fine, you go ahead. I'll be back out on the court in a few minutes." (*If* I lived!)

I continued pushing and felt a "pop" and I thought my insides would fall out if I took the plug out! "What the hell was *that?*" I wondered out loud to myself. Finally realizing I just couldn't stand it anymore, I pulled both of them out *s-l-o-w-l-y*. Thank the period gods, I had a quarter and went to the vending machine and got the old familiar sanitary pads and left the bathroom the same way I came in—well, not *exactly* the same! That's it, girls. That's how your mom lost her virginity!

We girls of the early sixties were still quite modern though compared to my grandmother who told me that as a girl, she had to use rags and they would wash them out after using them, and then hang them out on a clothes line to dry for the next time. Of course she had to make sure there were no boys around while the rags were hanging on the line! Do you suppose that's where the dirty little boys got the phrase, "she's on the rag" from? *Yuck*!

When they were finally invented, it took me a while to get used to panty liners. One time I excused myself from the table of an exclusive restaurant to go to the "ladies room" when my husband and I were out for dinner with friends. When I tried to pull my panties down...*it stuck to my pubes! I had put the panty liner on upside down!* The first panty liners weren't as "removable" as they are now, (this was pre-post-it glue era), but at least I didn't have to wear those darn sanitary belts that bite my butt anymore. It hurt like *Hell* when I pulled it off! After comparing it to a band-aid, (do I pull it off quickly or bit-by-bit?), I decided to bravely give it a high-speed tug...And there I was...leaning my head up against the cool steel toilet paper dispenser to "take a break" yet one more time after my very first Australian, (down under), bikini trim. Band-Aids really *did* stick back then!

Episodes like these were only the first indication that God's revenge against Eve and all her decedents was totally unfair. All of this because Eve liked apples and Adam was too stupid to resist her temptation! Some things *never* change! Men still blame women for everything!

This all made the explanation "God created man in His own image" clearer as time passed. Where did He come up with this whole period thing anyway? Whose side was Satan on? After all, Eve took the apple from *him*. It was *his* idea in the first place! Did *he* ever have a period? If he did, maybe that could be a realistic reason why he was so darn evil!

I will never eat apples again!

Men will *never* understand! I <u>very</u> briefly had a male roommate and the "unfairness-of-it-all" discussion came up. "I think the whole thing stinks!" I said.

"What stinks?" he asked.

"It stinks that women have to have the darn cramps and periods, then have to give birth and 8 times out of 10 raise the children by themselves and if *that* isn't enough, God hits us with menopause! It's just not fair!" I replied vehemently.

He was silent for a short while and was counting on his fingers. He finally said, "I figure women have about 420 periods in a lifetime. That doesn't seem so bad!"

"And how many have you had, you son of a bleep?"

He moved out shortly after that! Like I needed this.

CHAPTER TWO

Weddgies and Other Surprises

Until my early thirties, my biological life seemed somewhat non-eventful other than having my two daughters, until one day when my slacks started riding up my crotch. No, gentlemen. That does *not* feel good!

The Second Sign of Aging. I still had a taut tummy even after the two babies, but without warning, my butt *was starting to sag!* Wedgies were born. No more junior sizes for me. Junior sizes were for tight butts and girdles just weren't "in" anymore. (I bet you *still* don't understand what a girdle is! Google it!) *Bring on the polyester Misses Sizes with the elastic waists!* Like ugh...my mother's.

I mourned for the loss of my tight butt and began a lifetime battle of the bulge by purchasing my first of many in-home exercise machines. I spent a lot of time looking at my behind in the mirror and holding it up with my hands and letting it drop again. The older I got the farther and faster it dropped. But, just like you girls are thinking right now, I thought to myself, *"I'm sure I can beat this thing!"*

I began doing "butt tucks" every time I had to wait in a check-out line. I had read that you could do "butt tucks" anywhere and no one would be the wiser! Great!! I no longer looked for the shortest check-out line! I even did them in church during the sermon and while talking on the phone.

Exercise, exercise, exercise!

With two small children and a full-time job, I shouldn't have had the time to worry about what I looked like from behind, but I did anyway. Very vain of me, don't you think? After all, my husband already had a beer gut and had lost the hair on his head but was showing signs of it reappearing in his ears! But, *his butt didn't sag!* In fact, he didn't have much of a butt at all! The gap in the fairness scale widened. . .right along with my butt!

Exercise, exercise, exercise!

Many years later, the butt horror resurfaced. I was expecting a visit from an out-of-state old boyfriend. Check list: Girls are gone for the weekend, house is clean, hair is perfect, skin is soft, breasts and butt firm from 75 laps of swimming a week . . .and then while I was in front of the mirror, I turned around and applied scented body lotion to my back and my *butte. . .*

"Oh, My Gawd!" Where did all that cellulite come from? And the huge dimples? They looked like moon craters! I nearly screamed out loud. How often do *you* look at your backside in a mirror? Don't bother. It's very painful! You see the front side of you all the time in the mirror. That's how cellulite on your butt sneaks up on you literally behind your back. It's there before you know what to do about it and after it's there for a couple of years. . .there's not a darn thing you can do about it. It now has *Seniority!*

"What on earth can I do about this *now?* My date will be here in less than an hour." I said to myself. "Nothing could be done in this short of time and if *ever*", I thought to myself. Come up with Plan B.

Plan B was to make sure my date didn't see my backside naked in the light. Do you suppose he wondered why I either made him go up the stairs to the bedroom first or that whenever I was in front of him, I would walk backwards and incessantly talk to his face? All you girls know that candlelight is to hide all your imperfections. That's what "mood lighting" is all about! *"Thank the Lord for the nighttime"* took on new meaning.

I got away with *that* one without too much drama, but had to start preparing for the next time I would be caught naked and walking in front of someone! More research, more reading, drinking more water, creams, lotions, rubs, and of course, exercise, exercise, exercise. Seems no matter how hard I tried, Mother Time was always one step ahead of me.

I hate to be the bearer of bad news, but sagging butts and wedgies are inevitable and never go away unless you turn into an even bigger fanatic than I was. It's a lifetime sentence.

CHAPTER THREE

Body and Facial Hair

"All the other girls are doing it!" I yelled at my mother. "If they all jumped off a pier into the lake, would you do that too?" she yelled back. (That was one of her favorite ones!)

Not wanting to be different, I locked the bathroom door to shave my legs for the first time. "No one will notice anyway-especially my mother!" I said to myself.

I knew my dad kept his safety razor in the medicine cabinet in the upstairs bathroom. I don't know why they called it a "safety razor". Dad cut himself and came out of the bathroom with toilet paper dots on his face on a regular basis! Anyway, I climbed up on the bathroom sink and carefully took the safety razor out of the medicine cabinet. I opened it, shut it, open it, and shut it…just to get an idea of how it worked. I put in a brand new razor, (mistake number one) and filled the tub with hot water and bubbles, (I thought the bubbles would help), and climbed in the bathtub. Since I was doing this behind my mother's back, I sure couldn't ask *her* for advice! And I'll bet my sister *still* didn't shave her legs either because she always listened to my mother! She never did anything wrong!

Before I tried this little experiment, I asked some of the girls in school and they said they used really hot water, made a lot of lather from a bar of soap in their hands, smoothed the lather over their legs and started to shave."

Okay….Ivory Soap should be gentle enough for the first time. Definitely not the Lava my brothers used! I "lathered up" and raised one leg out of the water and propped it up with the heel of my foot on the corner of the bathtub. Just seconds before I put the razor against my leg… "I need the bathroom! What are you doing in there?"

My brother!

"I'm taking a bath! Use the downstairs bathroom!" "No!" the little rat said. He *knew* I was in the bathtub. He certainly heard the bath water running! All he really wanted to do was see me naked!

"Well you aren't coming in *this* bathroom. Go downstairs!"

"*Mommmm!*" he yelled running down the stairs. "I guess I'd better hurry!" I mumbled to myself. "Little rat!"

My leg was on an angle since I had bent the lower leg at the knee and it was now right in front of my face. (I was extremely agile back then.) Not familiar with this whole thing, the Ivory Soap made my legs *and* my hands slippery and my leg slipped from my grasp and dropped a little as I made my very first stroke.

I didn't feel anything at first-but I saw a hunk of dead skin hanging on the razor blades and within seconds blood started pouring out of my shin and into the bathtub. Did you know that blood makes bubbles disappear? Now the water was turning pink! "What do I do? What do I do?" *Can't panic!*

"What do I do? What do I do?"

I grabbed one of my dad's thick white socks that was lying on the floor where they weren't supposed to be, and used it as a tourniquet. I wasn't getting light-headed or anything, but no one should lose this much blood! There were hardly any bubbles left and the water was bright pink and getting cold!

I drained the barely hairy but now bloody water from the tub and sat there in the cold empty tub until the bleeding stopped. I finally removed the sock and found I had made a permanent "C" on my right shin. "No doubt it will scar and I will have it for the rest of my life!!" I said to myself under my breath.

"Are you done in there yet?" We had five kids. This time it was my little sister. "I'll be out in a minute!" Use the downstairs bathroom!" I yelled.

"Butch is in there!" "*Mommmm!* She screamed. "Barbie won't let me use the bathroom and I have to go really bad!"

I finally got dressed and ran limping into my bedroom. The bleeding had completely stopped by now, but I only had shaved my right shin. I guess I'll have to wait until my leg heels before I try this again! I'll have to wear long skirts every day to school. (Slacks on girls were not permitted in school yet). I waited until everyone was asleep and I snuck outside to put my dad's bloody white sock in the burn barrel. The next night at dinner, my dad said, "Betty, have you been using my razor for your legs again?" He was mad and I kept my mouth shut and kept eating. "And I'm missing one of my white socks", he continued. "There was only one in the bathroom! I wish you would keep better track of them when you do the laundry!" I still kept my mouth shut!

The next time I tried shaving my legs I was a bit more successful and the next time and the next time even better. I was so sure my mother never noticed my smooth legs but for Christmas there was a brand new electric Lady Schick for me under the tree! Bless her discreteness!

One *good* thing I have discovered as I got older, the hair on your legs doesn't grow as fast as when you are younger. You no longer have

15

to shave every day. It's just not there. Or…is it that you just don't see it as well?

ROUGE HAIRS

I was resting peacefully on my college-age daughter's bed while she took a shower during one of her visits home. We always talked in her bedroom while she unpacked and I guess I dozed off. I woke up in excruciating pain and grabbed for my chin! I opened my eyes to see my daughter leaning over me with a pair of tweezers in her hand and grinning from ear-to-ear.

"Those two hairs on your chin have been driving me *crazy!*" she said.

"*What* hairs?" I yelled as I was rubbing my chin. She directed me into the bathroom and showed me the remaining two hairs left on my chin in the magnified mirror! "*Oh! My Gawd!* How long have *those* been there?"

"For quite a while," she said. I can't believe you didn't see them yourself! They were driving me crazy!"

(They were so tiny, how could I? The eyes were getting bad too!) "Take them off! Take them off!" I yelled in disgust. So I lay back down on the bed and she extracted the two remaining hairs-one more on my chin and a really long curly one below my chin on my neck.

"This one is long enough to curl", she said as she laughed. I sneered! And I wanted to throw up! Maybe all that water and vitamin E were fertilizing the hair on my face! *Now* what do I do? What she didn't know, is that I had already plucked a few rogue hairs from my breast nipples. No one could see those except me and that's something she just didn't need to know!

So that began my chin plucking era. If I forgot to check in the magnified mirror regularly and felt a rogue hair on my chin while I was stuck in traffic, I got pretty good at pulling them out with my finger nails. You *know* you got it because it really hurts!

Now here's where one of life's most rewarding blessings come in. That same daughter, now 39, complained to me one day about the darn hairs on her chin and how brittle and stubborn they are! I think it just slipped out of her mouth by accident. She *knew* what I was thinking the minute she said it.

Not so funny when the shoe's on the other foot, is it? No sympathy here!

BIKINI WAXES

A few years later, my youngest daughter was learning how to remove hair with hair wax removal at her job in a beauty shop. She asked me if she could use me for practice doing bikini waxes. "Sure" I said. "Anything for science."

I wasn't at all sure what a bikini wax was, but what the heck, she had to learn from someone and why not her unsuspecting mother? "Let's go into the bathroom. The hot wax is already hot and ready to apply."

"*Hot wax?*" I went into the bathroom. "Now pull your panties down." "Do What?" She repeated, "Pull your panties down. I *told* you, we're going to do a *bikini wax.*"

I sat on the toilet seat, leaning against the back of the toilet with my panties around my ankles in a position I never thought she would see me in and she began applying the wax. It was a little warm and uncomfortable but she said it needed to be that warm. Then she placed little cloth strips over the glued areas. "It has to sit a few minutes to soften the hair," she said.

By this time, my other daughter came home from work. "Tracy, hurry upstairs! I'm giving mom a bikini wax and I am just about ready to pull the strips off!"

By the speed at which Tracy dropped everything she was carrying and flew up the stairs, I was wondering if I should have signed a medical release form before I did this. Now both daughters were in the bathroom watching me naked from the waist down, sitting on the toilet seat. They just looked at each other and smiled, rather diabolically, I thought. "Time's up. Are you ready?" Trish asked.

Ready? Ready for *what?* Maybe I should have asked more questions before this started! Too late! She R-I-P-P-E-D off the first cloth strip-along with the first layer of my skin! "I'd rather go through childbirth!" I yelled. "Don't do any more! It hurts!"

She ripped off another one...and another one! She and her sister were laughing hysterically! Why, oh why, did they get such enjoyment from their mother's pain? Didn't I sacrifice enough when I gave birth? Never, ever again, will I put myself through that *or* give my daughters so much pleasure at my expense!

After the waxing episode, in my never-ending search for the perfect hair removal remedy, I purchased a hair extractor. This technological wonder, no doubt created by a masochistic man with a sick, sick mind, "pulled" the hair out by the root so the hairs would take longer to grow back. I read all the instructions and started on my legs. *My Gawd!* It hurt! I could hear the motor "zing" like an electronic bug zapper, as it mechanically pulled each hair out! Bits of hair and skin would fly out from under the extractors like grass blades from a lawn mower. Those faded from my sight after the tears in my eyes blurred my vision. I stopped and looked for signs of bleeding. I read the warning directions once again and nowhere, N-O-W-H-E-R-E did the directions say anything about *excruciating pain!*

I started again, sure I would get used to it. More zinging, more pain, still no blood, but I persisted until I had at least one-half of the first leg done. I felt my skin. It really *did* feel smooth like the package claimed. But how much *smooth* could a woman take?

I read the directions again. In fine print, the instructions indicated that you would have to let the hair grow out to a considerable length so the hair extractor had something to grab the next time you removed the hair. (*Next* time?) The manufacturer promised I would have smooth legs for about the first ten days. After that, your legs would look like a French woman's armpits before you could "extract" again. The hair wouldn't be too noticeable at first, the bristles would just stick to your panty hose until it got long enough to be smooth and lay down flat. *Then* you could extract again. *Baloney!* Something deep inside me said, "Don't do this again or you will *die*!" I grabbed my own safety razor and finished the job and then packed the nearly new hair extractor neatly back into the box. I had a wonderful idea…I would give it to my daughters as a gift for Christmas and then return the favor of watching *them* in pain just as they had watched me getting my bikini wax! Revenge is Sweet!

HAIR IN OTHER UNUSUAL PLACES

About the time hair begins growing in "unusual places", the eyesight begins to fade. This in itself is a blessing.

I could no longer give myself a pedicure without the aid of my bifocals so I grabbed my nail kit and of course, my bifocals and sat down to give myself a pedicure. Since this was the first time I used my glasses for the task, I was shocked when I saw 5 or 6 black, bristly hairs protruding out of my big toes. *"Oh, how gross! Where did those come from and how long have they been there?"* Do I shave them off… or pluck them?

Plucking would last longer. Let's try that. I grabbed the tweezers. Little did I know that my toes were much more sensitive than the eyebrows I had been plucking for thirty years. The first "pluck" brought tears to my eyes! I tried another and again, I couldn't see anymore because of the tears in my eyes. I hesitated. Composed myself and once again, was saved by the safely razor.

But you know what? You have more wrinkles on your toes that you do on your legs, (exception—above the knees after sixty!). I sliced the top of the first toe with the razor. Now I had a big toe that was bright pink from the plucking and bleeding from the sharp razor. I wiped off the blood, put the razor down, took my glasses off and just sat there on the bathroom floor contemplating my next move. I think that is enough for today.

Plucking hurts. Maybe I should ice them first-you know, like when you have your ears pierced but I could only imagine the jabbing I would get from my daughters if they came home and saw me sitting on the bathroom floor with ice cubes on my big toes! In order to shave them with a safety razor, you must have to curl your toes under so the wrinkles stretch away before you can shave them. I guess I was still in shock that I actually had hair on my toes anyway and all of this was just too much for my mid-forty brain!

I put everything away and like Scarlett, "I'll think about it tomorrow." I had one clean, pink, bloody big toe and one big toe with hair on it. I would wear socks for a few days and try again later. Good decision!

THE BRIGHTER SIDE

Unfortunately, I developed neuropathy in my late fifties, but God always gives you a silver lining. It took me a while to become aware of this particular blessing. Neuropathy is a very painful neurological disorder that deadens the nerves and is treated with muscle relaxants and pain killers. I found out that I can now pluck the hairs from my big toes and *I just don't feel it!* Irony of it all is that over sixty, you just don't care anymore and wear tennis shoes, so no one can tell you if hair is growing on your toes or not! Double jeopardy.

Speaking about body hair and bifocals, isn't it amazing that Our Maker decided that most body hair doesn't arrive until *after* our eyesight diminishes? I think this was His master plan to trick couples into thinking their partners were still perfect in their own eyes. Imagine what damage could be done at the first sighting of hair protruding from the inside and back of the ears and the nose and on the big toes? So, there goes the eyesight and the partner just doesn't "see" it! What do you suppose His plan is about beer bellies? I could have used that one!

EYEBROWS

Plucking your eyebrows is a necessary evil. Not that mine were ever very bushy, but they were dark brown and cleaning up strays underneath them became a ritual because face powder and eye shadow tend to cake around the annoying little buggers. I never had enough excess strays to warrant eye brow waxing, which from my bikini wax and hair extractor sagas made me feel extremely fortunate, but I really couldn't go around with spotted eye lids. Regardless, I would wait until I really needed a trim before I grabbed the tweezers and magnifying glass.

I don't care what anyone says. This really hurts! I would ice the lids first and then pluck them out. The ice helped the initial pain but didn't do anything about the red puffy lids that would hang around a day or two. I wore my glasses on those days to cover it up.

I believe the first time I plucked my eyebrows was my senior year in high school. My mother, of course said I didn't need to do it. "The natural look was so much prettier." She said. But then mom didn't shave her arms *or* her legs on a regular basis either!

"Yeah, right" I thought. I was beginning to feel like a Neanderthal!

So just like shaving my legs with a safety razor for the first time, I plucked my eyebrows behind her back-as usual. Well, just like the leg shaving incident, I got caught-again. I plucked my right eyebrow too far into the arch of the brow and I had a "no hair zone". So *now* what do I do? I was planning on getting my senior pictures taken soon and now I had a bald spot in my eyebrows. Like a fool, I asked dear old mom if she would buy me an eyebrow pencil.

"Out of the question!" she said. "You made your bed. You lie in it!" (Another one of her favorite sayings.)

So I went to one of her "cool friends" and asked her to get me an eyebrow pencil. She took me to the store and not only bought me one but showed me how to use it! I am sure my mother noticed but she never said anything and I never squealed on her girlfriend. You never know when you'll need another partner in crime!

Here's a bit of good news…as you get older, the strays finally give up and wear out from years of plucking and just quit growing. (Or is it I can't see them as well?). But, and it's a big but, the eyebrows themselves get bushier to get even! All that calcium has to go somewhere, after all!

After 55 or so, you have to start thinning the eyebrows from where else-the top. Easy do-no plucking, no pain. You just take a fine toothed comb and comb the brows upward. With the long hairs still in the comb, take your free hand to take a pair of small finger nail scissors and trim off the excess to the natural brow line. Done! Just don't take too much off. It takes a little practice but well worth it. Add that little tip to the eyebrow coloring coming up in the next chapter and you have twenty-five-year-old eyebrows on a sixty-year-old face!! There must be a balance in there somewhere.

CHAPTER FOUR

Gray Hair

I vaguely remember having my hair frosted silver when I was 18 years old. It took hours in the beauty shop to remove all the color from my naturally dark brown hair but somehow I thought it made my complexion look softer. Everyone was doing it and it was "cool" until the dark roots started growing in and I didn't want to go through that process again. I went back to my natural dark hair. *Dark* roots. Oh, how I pray for them now that they have turned to silver!

When I was about 28 years old, my sister-in-law took great pleasure in finding a gray hair on the back of my head. I always loved my dark brown hair, but it was easy to see that hiding gray hair would be more difficult than if I had blonde hair. After she left, I pulled out my hand mirror and searched layer by layer, root by root. It didn't take long to find four solid gray-to-the-root hairs that I rapidly pulled out.

"Ouch! That hurt!" Not quite as bad as the big toe hairs, but the tugs definitely did not feel good! Sometime later, I read that for every gray hair you pull out, two grow back in! Can't do *that* anymore. I guess I must have pulled one too many gray hairs out and since they double each time you do or so "they" say, deception failed me because my mother one day spotted several gray hairs in my colic at the temple of my head. She was horrified! "What the hell is *that?*" she screamed as she hit me smack on the forehead! "You are too young to have gray hair! *I'm* too young to have a daughter that has gray hair! *Dye it!*" she said in frustration!

She was devastated? My aging process made *her* feel old. I was horrified too and now my head hurt where she smacked me! I couldn't really understand my mother's reaction until I got older and *my* daughters made me feel old every chance they got which they did on as many occasions as possible.

I was going to the gym three days a week for aerobics and free weights, (to fight the sagging butt syndrome), and became good friends with another lady who most likely had bagging butt syndrome too. We started talking about the gray hair dilemma after class one day. After a few tears and heartfelt girl talk, I asked Debbie to go to the drug store with me and help me pick out my first box of hair color. I decided that nobody would ever know when I "went gray". For crying-out-loud, I was only thirty! If I remember correctly, there were probably only two brands available at that time. Fewer choices equal fewer painful decisions when I went to the drug store to buy my hair color. This part was a snap!

Regardless, I was still a nervous wreck about coloring my hair. I needed to "wash that gray right out of my hair" before my husband got home. He had lost all his hair years ago, but for some reason, I didn't want him to know I was going gray. Go figure? I read the directions at least 3 times. I know girls, I am really slow sometime-even way back then! I had all the ingredients and the directions laid out on the bathroom sink and read the directions one more time, took a deep breath and began.

I think I splashed hair color all over the bathroom…the walls, the sink, the toilet, the floor. "How the heck was I going to get this mess cleaned up before my husband got home at 4:00?" It didn't look this hard when they did it on TV. I was afraid to leave the bathroom once I got it applied or I would get the dye on everything I touched and left a trail everywhere I walked. So I sat on the toilet, waiting for the time to pass before I could rinse it out. The t-shirt I was wearing was designated as my hair-color-dying shirt forever after my first application. What else do you think about sitting on a toilet waiting for 40 minutes to pass?

Already a mess, I had no idea the worst was yet to come! As I leaned my head over the bathroom sink, I could see the solution splashing from the corner of the one eye I hadn't gotten the brown ooze into yet! Dark brown was all over. I was grateful that the curtains were already dark brown and I was trying so hard to be careful! "How the heck am I going to get this cleaned up before 4:00?"

I got into the shower to finish rinsing so now I had the brown goop all over the shower too. When I thought I was finished, I grabbed a towel. "Oops! I guess it wasn't all rinsed out yet!" It was all over the towel now too. Back into the shower! The towel was designated to be my hair dying towel now, along with the t-shirt. There couldn't have been much solution left in my hair, so I was certain I was done. I blow dried my hair and looked into the mirror. "Hey. It looks pretty good! I don't think anyone will ever notice!" I said confidently.

"But look at this mess!" It was 3:45! I spun around the bathroom like Mrs. Clean scrubbing everything until it shined. I took the towel and t-shirt out to the dumpster deciding I didn't want the evidence around after all and walked back into the house. Who knows if I'll ever have the courage to do this again anyway? Then I took the gloves off. How in the heck did the dye get under my finger nails inside the gloves? "Oh, well." It was 3:55. Just enough time to bleach my nails! My husband walked in promptly at 4:00. "What's that smell?" he asked. "Never thought about the smell." I said to myself!

"And what's that brown mark on the back of your neck? What have you been doing?" Caught like a rat! Oh, well. It's always hard doing something for the first time. You know, riding a bike, roller skating, sex, and now add, coloring your hair...!

So I have been coloring my hair for over 30 years now. I have it down to a science. At one time I even got creative and decided *not* to color my sideburns and let the gray show naturally through. *My gawd, my hair wasn't gray, it was white!* That experiment lasted only one month after a male friend of mine asked, "Do you color your hair?"

"Me? No. This is natural. Why do you ask?" Well, it's so white around your ears; I thought I'd suggest you start coloring your hair." he said. Men are so stupid and I was just beginning to like this guy!! Have you ever known a one of them who knows just how to make a woman feel good about herself?

So I went back to "*naturally* dark brown" (sideburns and all), from then on. So much for creative! Now, right after I color the roots, I wait twenty minutes and then comb it through to the ends so it has highlights and my hair hasn't fallen off yet!

My next traumatic gray hair event happened when I was about 50. I found a thick, stubborn gray hair in my right eyebrow. Yes, girls, your eyebrows *do* go gray along with the rest of it. By the time I spotted it with my ever weakening eyesight, it was curling upwards. It was so thick and coarse that it was difficult to pluck, but pluck I did. Well, I got it after I missed and pulled a few healthy natural brown hairs first. I just wasn't ready for this. It hurt like hell and actually bled. Blot, blot, and blot...what happened to the large pores I used to have? Where are they when I need them?

After 60, my eyebrows were going bald from plucking! The no-longer-gray-hairs-but-white-hairs were coming in faster than I could pluck them. I never did care for my grandmother plucking out all her eyebrows and then drawing a pencil-thin line in the shape of eyebrows. So here's what I did, and I haven't died or gone blind yet! I had been warned from several hairdressers to never color my eyebrows myself- that it was too dangerous. *"Don't try this at home!"* But then they wanted me to come to them to have my hair colored too instead of doing it myself. That was hardly ever in my budget either, so I confidently started coloring my own eyebrows. After coloring my hair, I squeeze a little hair color on a cotton swab and *carefully* apply my hair color to my eyebrows every <u>other</u> time I color. (Eyebrows don't grow as fast as the hair on your head!) After taking a comb with small teeth and combing it through, I then take a moist cotton swab and wipe off any excess. I leave it on until I rinse it out the same time I rinse the color from my hair. I was amazed at how much younger I looked the first time I did it! No regrets here. New Victory in the fight against aging!

I don't recommend this for everyone or I'd be sued by the first woman who got hair color in her eyes and went blind. This is just what I do and I love it! The first time I did it, I was a bit scared, but I didn't poke my eye out either. It took ten years off my life and I'm going to keep on doing it until I can't lift my hands to my forehead anymore!

There were many, many times that I looked for gray pubes but I haven't found one yet. Well, I haven't looked very hard either. There was a time I used my bifocals and a magnifying glass for a pube inspection because I may have thought when I find one of those, it would be time to give it up! After all, no one has figured out that I color my hair in all this time! *Yeh...right!* Maybe I gave up looking because men my age have poor eyesight too and who would want the lights on at my age if a man *would* get that close? But most of all, I have this little roll between my belly button and my pubes now and I just can't see it. Most realistically, it's because I really don't care anymore!

So, back to the top of matter... (I'm talking about my head again). I suppose the next stage is when and *how* to let it go totally gray when the time comes. Like if my arms fall off and I can no longer reach my head or they find out all hair color causes cancer!

I *did* come close to taking the plunge the year I turned sixty. Not long after I mastered the eyebrow thing, I tried on silver wigs one day when I was shopping with my daughter. (Hmmm. Didn't look too bad.) I didn't actually buy one, I was just curious to see what I would look like in silver hair. Armed with a little more bravery seeing what I could potentially look like, I paid a beautician in one of the most exclusive shops in Scottsdale, $400 to strip all the color from my hair. When she finished, I asked for a mirror. She hesitated. "I'm not sure you want to see this. Sometimes this happens on dark hair colors," she said sheepishly.

"Give me the mirror, you coward!" My hair was not gray or white or anything in-between. It was *orange!* "You've just been through a serious illness," she continued, "and you're not 100% back on your feet yet. Maybe you should wait a while, like when you are feeling better, before you decide to go gray," she had the nerve to continue! Or like when Hell freezes over!

"Gray Hell-this is *orange and a very ugly orange at that!*" I hadn't been *that* sick that I couldn't tell the difference between gray and light, dirty orange! I was furious! But I had to pay the four hundred bucks anyway and I walked out of the shop covering my head. My daughters thought this was hilarious! (They always did have a lousy sense of humor!) I wore a scarf or a ball cap or just stayed in my bedroom for three long weeks before it was safe enough for me to color my hair brown again. So much for going natural! I've been coloring my hair for thirty years now. Thirty more won't make that much of a difference!

I have met so many women my age who look beautiful in white hair and I really admire them for their courage! Occasionally, I got tempted to try again until I ask them how they did it. Worse response was, "Well, I had chemo and when it grew back it actually grew back in curly too, so I decided not to color it anymore." I don't plan on having chemo, by the grace of God and I've been without curly hair my entire life, so why start that way? Besides going orange or getting cancer, another method is to let it grow out naturally or shave my head bald, and then wear a wig, a ball cap or a scarf for two years until it grows out! I thought three weeks was bad! *Two years? That's insane!*

I remember being in shock when I saw my mother the first time with all-white hair! We lived half-way across our country from each other and I hadn't seen her in over two years. Before I moved from Charleston, SC to Phoenix, Arizona, I visited my mother in Ohio. I walked in the door and the first thing I said was, "Mother! When did you quit coloring your hair?" No dark ends with silver roots, she was totally white at 67 years old! (Kind of like me when you think about it). My mother had always dyed her hair coal black! I guess if I had been around while she went through the process of letting it go natural, I would have had time to get used to it. But, for me, she went from black to white! And this is just one more reason why I am writing this book. She never told me about going from black to white!

I *promise* not to do that to you girls! In fact, I will make a pact with you. You can take turns coloring my hair for me after my arms no longer reach my head, or they really do fall off! Just be careful not to get it all over the bathroom!"

I recently visited my lovely, ninety-two-old aunt in Ohio. She still colors her own hair, applies make-up every day, meticulously cleans her own house and dresses beautifully with shoes and jewelry to match. If she can do it, I can do it! *"Aunt Mary Alice is my new Idol!*

"Natural" brown stays! Sideburns, eyebrows and all! Changed my mind and chickened out yet one more time. Well, for now anyway.

OKAY, IT'S TIME

I don't know if age makes you wiser or you just finally look reality dead in the eye and say, "Okay, it's time". Just before my 64th birthday, I finally bit the bullet for real this time. All my promises to myself to stay dark brown for the rest of my life aside, I was tired of coloring, touching up and worrying about it. The silver roots grew in faster and faster until I was coloring every three weeks. I used a temporary color on the roots the last week. I could see the icy white roots and it made me shiver! I had been coloring my hair for over thirty years by the time I made this earth shattering decision. I was tired of it but just couldn't make the decision to throw the hair color out the window, put my big girl panties on and go silver-I was *certain* it was silver. Or was it? Was it instead a murky dull gray or dried up yellow?

Letting my hair grow out naturally was a big, life changing decision. "If I didn't like it, I could always color it again." I told myself. But by that time, everyone would know I was gray anyway, so what the heck good would that do? Drove me crazy!

My dark brown hair was beyond shoulder length, all one length the first time in my life and looked youthful, full and healthy. I decided to go curly, first with bobby pins every night for a month or two, (did you ever sleep on bobby pins?) Before long, I really got used to the new style and decided on a permanent. I used to give them to myself all the time when I was younger so I went to the discount beauty supply center nearby and had them help me pick out a permanent and permanent rollers. "Have you ever done this yourself?" they asked. "Do it all the time." I lied. Don't know what went wrong, but my hair got burned

31

to the root and my beautiful youthful, full and healthy, all one length, dark brown hair started falling out by the brush full! This happened to me once before when my uncle's boyfriend, a master hair stylist in Palm Springs who didn't like me, gave me a permanent in the exclusive salon he worked in. The only way to fix it then was to cut it as short as possible and let it grow out again. Well, if I had to go short again, I may as well take letting it grow out gray into consideration. Two birds with one hairy stone, you know. Chickened out yet one more time.

Finally my daughter showed me some really cute short hair styles she pulled up online and showed me several articles on how to let your hair go natural. The visions of me looking like my silver-haired grandmother, (lovely as she was), with short, permanent-waved silver hair, Saturday mornings at the hair dresser and sleeping in a hair net every night of week and a new permanent every three months started to fade. Some of these short hair styles were absolutely adorable-silver and all! With encouragement from my daughter, I was beginning to weaken as I cleaned my brush out one more time and threw a fistful of permanent-damaged dark hair in the waste basket.

Maybe it really is time.

My daughter made the hair appointment for me and told me she would go with me for support. Yep. It was time, but I was scared to death. Perhaps having a partner in my crime made it a little easier so I wouldn't chicken out. I sat in the car next to her, looked at her, and wondered how brave she would be when *she* had to make this decision. Would it be so casual then? Time wouldn't be on her side forever!

I finally chose a hair style and with picture in hand, I climbed into the beautician chair. My hair was only about 2" on the top when she finished. It was cropped above the ears and shaved up the back. *I mean extremely short! You talk about a nervous hair dresser!* Before she started, she asked me, "Are you sure?" Then she took a "Before picture". Two other beauticians covered the big mirror in front of me. (Like a black bag over the head of someone about to be hanged?) Next came the scissors and clippers. When she finished, I ran my fingers through my hair for the first time and thought to myself, "At least all the nasty permanent was gone and the roots feel like real hair again." I couldn't see it myself since they still had the mirror covered.

I looked down on the floor to see my shorn dark brown locks and there wasn't anything there. "We swept it up while we were cutting so you wouldn't have to see it and get upset", she explained. "Oh", I said. Like not having any mirrors or hair on the floor would keep me from feeling I may have just made the biggest mistake in my life. *"Mirror... Now!"*

And there it was-the new me. Mirrors don't lie. I still had dark brown tips but surprisingly I *liked* the short hairstyle! Three stylists and my daughter were standing motionlessly around me waiting for the bomb to go off but I surprised myself and them by honestly declaring, "I think I like it!" They nearly applauded from relief!!

The deed was done! Stage one was a success!

The next day I told everyone that I was letting the gray grow in—I think I made the announcement so I wouldn't chicken out and reach for the hair color again. Everyone I knew was so supportive and told me how much they loved my new hairstyle. That really helped you know, the up-frontedness and the support!

I used temporary hair color on the roots for about three months. After two more trims, I was able to stop using that because most of the dark brown was gone. It just looked like I had my hair tipped with the darker color. That was a day to celebrate because I could throw the temporary color bottle in the trash! All together, it took about eight months, (not two years), before the last strains of brown were gone and I decided I really liked the new me.

My goodness! Why had I make such a big deal of this?

So my silver haired lady stage began and I haven't regretted a day of it! The silver and gray hair seems to soften my facial features-just like it did when I was eighteen. Wrinkles don't seem as obvious as they did with the contrast of the artificial dark brown and I've had so many kind people tell me the color makes me look younger! I happen to agree with them. Should have done it years ago! I am finally acting my age. Well, at least in most respects!

I didn't tell anyone back in Ohio about my transformation. I thought I would just surprise them the next time I visited-like my mother did to me! After being gray for nearly a year, my son-in-law took a picture of me, my daughter and granddaughter. It was a lovely picture, but two days later, I started getting phone calls from everyone back east asking, "When did you go gray?" My daughter had posted the photo on Facebook. So much for the surprise element!

So now, when I sit out on the patio and see my

image in the patio door, I say, *"Hello Mom"*.

CHAPTER FIVE

Wrinkles, Ages Spots and Craters

I always had exceptionally soft skin-a gift from my German ancestors I would imagine. I remember one time a classmate passed me in the locker room of the gym as we were getting dressed after gym class and she accidentally brushed her hand against my back as I was getting dressed. She called her twin sister over right away. "Feel the skin on Barbara's back! It feels like satin!" Marsha came over and so did about five other girls…all to feel the skin on my back. I felt absolutely weird. The whole thing freaked me out! It never happened again-that personal attention from other girls-so I decided I really liked the one-time attention and smiled to myself thinking while walking down the crowded hallways of my high school, 'Hey, you should feel my skin!"

Until then, I didn't know I had skin any different than anyone else. So I began taking more pride in my soft skin, putting lotion on it daily and taking baths in baby oil. I guess it made me feel special. That adolescence experience and the vain behavior pattern I developed from it probably prevented me from aging sooner so vanity *does* have its benefits! Even at the ripe old age of 65, I still have soft skin-there's quite a bit more of it now, but it's a doggone shame no one can appreciate it beside myself! I can only hope that my daughters have inherited the same genes and the same vanity but even more, I hope they have someone to share it with.

You can't expect to talk about skin and aging without expecting a discussion about my Next Apparent Affliction—*Wrinkles*.

My next door neighbor walked into my house one day unexpectedly. Judy had five children, was a part-time nurse and had a huge house to take care of. Five children make you awfully wise and I respected and loved her. When I heard her come in the back door, I yelled at her that I was in the living room. She walked in and found me lying on the couch with my feet propped up and two frozen spoons attached to my eyes. (This gives a whole new meaning to "spooning"). I kept the icy cold spoons on my eyes fifteen minutes a day and it had only been ten minutes. It wasn't time for me to get up yet.

"What in the hell are you doing?" she asked.

"I read this article about aging that said ice was the cure of premature wrinkling." I'm not so sure cryonics had been developed yet, but I'm sure it was the same theory.

"And since when do *you* have time to read…or lay on the couch with spoons on your eyes?"

"I read all about it in the doctor's office while I was waiting for my appointment." I explained. "The article said that if you apply ice to the wrinkled areas, they will disappear with little or no side effects and no surgery. I figured the best way to apply ice to my eyes was to freeze wet spoons and place them on my eyes a couple times a day. The spoons fit really well! It feels really good too. You ought to try it!"

"But you don't *have* any wrinkles! You're only 29 years old!" she said.

"Better late than never!"

For about a year I always had two spoons in the freezer preparing for my "treatment". Why at 29, it seemed to be working! Somewhere along the line, I let life happen as it tends to do as a Super Mom and I quit doing it. Maybe I should try it again!

Wrinkles around your eyes are the first to be noticeable. Some people call them "bird's feet", others call them "wisdom lines", and still others like to call the ones around your mouth "laugh lines". I don't see *anything* funny about any of them and I call them "*a pain in the behind*" because it's the first thing I see in the mirror every morning. You just can't pretend they are not there. As if they don't look bad enough, I would have to squint into the mirror to get the maximum effect and see exactly where they were and then walk directly to the freezer and get the spoons. What you don't realize is that these pesky little road maps start developing on <u>all</u> parts of your body sooner or later. You just don't notice them as easily as the ones on your face. They start in little discreet areas like the back of your neck, in your arm pits, and above your knees. The ones that really sneak up on you are the wrinkles on your wrists. Who would ever expect to have wrinkles on your wrists? (Get the lotion!). And to make things worse, if you don't exercise enough, wrinkles begin appearing in the folds of your butt and I don't believe they have spoons with the right contour or big enough for that, but somehow, you have to keep up with it all or the little buzzards will creep on you!

Another visit to the doctor and in another article, I read that you could prevent wrinkles by exercising your face. So the next time my neighbor walked into my house, she caught me making faces at myself in the mirror.

"*Now* what are you doing?" she asked.

"Exercising my face to prevent wrinkles," I answered. I do this *before* the spoons."

I later read that water, not oil, replenishes your skin. (Stop the oil baths right now!). So I bought a squirt bottle and began each day squirting my face and letting it dry by itself. "*Hmmm*," I said to myself. "If this works for my face, it must certainly work for my whole body!" So when no one else was home, I began squirting my entire body with water and walking around nude until my skin air dried.

Good grief! I hope Judy doesn't walk in right now. It was the dead of winter and only 28 degrees outside She might think I'm really nuts this time! (You think?)

MOISTURIZER

While my daughters were very young, I wanted to go back to work but needed something flexible so I would not miss out on any of their childhood milestones. I still wanted to be a hands-on mom, but my financial and mental independent side needed to be nurtured too. I became an in-home make-up and skin care consultant through an independent franchise owner in my home town. This move would lead me to the discovery of probably the single most essential piece of anti-aging advice I will be able to pass onto you. Moisturizer.

To become a consultant, I was trained on proper skin care and make-up application and of course, trained to sell *lots* of product and earn *lots* of money on my own schedule with Home Parties. You've all been to them-jewelry, pots and pans, Tupperware, toys, psychic parties, and on and on and on. At these parties, I would give the Hostess a Make-Over in front of their closest friends. (Had to be close, trusted friends because they would all see you in your worst no make-up face and had to be trusted not to tell everyone how awful you look without make-up.) First I gave a demonstration on proper cleansing and skin care before I applied the make-up to only one side of their faces. This was so the audience could see the "before" and "after" of these miraculous products I was selling. Of course after everyone "*Oohed*" and *"Ahhed"*, I would apply make-up to the naked side of the hostess's face to complete the Make-Over and then have her walk around the room to give everyone an opportunity to feel how soft her skin was. Then I would go over to my make-shift office on the kitchen table and start taking orders while they were hot! Sooner or later I would treat the hostess to makeup on the other side of her face and write up more orders.

Of course I had to wear the product myself-Truth in Advertising, you know. It didn't take me long to realize that the most valuable product in this or any other line of makeup was the moisturizer. You could tell the moment you applied dark circle concealer under your eyes whether or not you had applied moisturizer first. The concealer caked and matted as you literally dragged it onto your dry skin and that only caused more wrinkles. So you would stop and go back to apply the moisturizer and start over. I was only in my mid-twenties when I discovered this most important instrument of anti-aging. Until that time, I thought moisturizer was for dried up old skin. *Wrong!* You begin using moisturizer *before* your skin shows the affects of normal aging from every-day-stress, sun and wind damage and of course Mother Nature's wryly cruel sense of humor.

Back to the Truth in Advertising...a few months after I started this career, my face started breaking out and I found out I was *allergic* to the product! Ouch! So this job was scratched, but after seeing the importance of moisturizer, I found a hypo-allergenic brand and have used it every day my entire life. Can't say this is scientifically proven, but deep in my heart, I know that this single product has helped my skin stay younger looking. I started using moisturizer before the wrinkles came and I would advise you to do that same! How about twelve years old or so. Better yet-why don't we tie it in with puberty to be on the safe side!

In addition, I heard somewhere that you need to replenish the moisture in your skin from the "inside". That's when I became a "water preppie". I ordered purified water instead of a mixed drink when I went out and began carrying a bottle of water with me everywhere I went and that was before I moved to Arizona! I would drink water until I burst. Had I only known then that purified water would become the national drink, I would have bought stock!

A few years later, a woman I worked with told me that vitamin E and Fish Oil prevent wrinkles. So I bought vitamin E and Fish Oil and still take it today. They are much easier to take than a spray bottle and walking around the house in the nude. I took advice from anyone once the subject of wrinkles came up and a new treatment would come up all the time. Creams, mud masks, the "blue mask", eyeglass-shaped ice packs, massaging the chicken crow on your neck, and of course, exercise, exercise, exercise. I tried them all.

Funny how I could listen to any conversation about wrinkles and retain it all, yet I used to fall asleep in Algebra because I couldn't get excited about it. Talk about priorities!

All of this must have paid off because when I was over fifty, I went to a "Pimps and Prostitutes" party dressed in my daughter's skin-tight white leather body suit with a very low-cut back. One of the men I met there brushed his hand against my bare back as we talked and he finally asked me how old I was. (Don't think for a minute I was about to tell him!) When I wouldn't answer him, he asked me if I ever considered dating "older" men. (He had to be a whole 35 or 36 years old!)

"Why you must be only 28 or 29. I can tell *because of your skin!*" This brought back fond memories of that day in the girl's locker room and the very beginning of my soft skin obsession! I guess all my home remedies paid off or else he was extremely intoxicated! I like to think they just paid off!

PETROLIUM JELLY

I was nearly sixty when I discovered another valuable weapon in the fight against wrinkles. In Arizona, the weather is extremely dry—you know, the "dry heat" we talk about. Although it helps us tolerate temperatures above 110 degrees a minimum of four months out of the year, it also dries out your skin which is probably the single most dreaded cause of aging in the desert. I needed a single most miraculous solution. Besides drinking a lot of water, I have used lip balm on my lips since moving to Arizona. It's hard to keep anything out here moist-especially your lips. While using it on my lips one hot, dry day, for some unusual reason I remembered a television advertisement that was popular when I was much younger. It showed someone gently rubbing lip balm all over a dried leaf. After a few hours, the leaf was green and healthy again. *"If ChapStick can do this for a leaf, imagine what it could do for your chapped lips!"*

Well, why not? If it worked miracles on the leaves and veins of that dried up old leaf, why not use it on my "veins"-my wrinkles! So instead of applying it exclusively to my dry lips, I extended it to the top and bottom of my lips before I went to bed at night to get rid of the "smoker's lines" I had been getting. Look a little farther. Why not the crow's feet around my eyes and the laugh lines? Gradually, I was applying a generous amount of lip balm on those areas of my face and it was working but I was going through a lot of lip balm!

Before moving to Arizona, I used petroleum jelly on my dried and cracked heels and feet when they got out of control in the winter months when I lived in the mid west.. I would apply a generous amount on my feet and put socks on before I went to bed. By morning, they were much smoother. After a few nights, my feet were pretty again. Since I already had a big jar of petroleum jelly in my nightstand, (for my feet, of course!), I started using that instead of so much lip balm.

Guess what? It worked and I've shared this secret with only my closest girlfriends. I'm throwing this little tip in for free, but don't let the low price fool you. Petroleum jelly is one of my biggest defense products in my battle against wrinkles!

As I got older, I got a wrinkle tip from my daughter. At the final fitting of her sleeveless wedding gown, she noticed little folds of skin with "Oh-my-gawd" wrinkles under her arms. Being only thirty, she was in shock! She freaked! "Oh, my god, I'm only 30 years old! Where did *those* come from? Mom! What can I do? I can't go down the aisle with wrinkles in my armpits!"

"Who, me? Like I am an expert in the Wrinkle Department?" I said. I didn't know she had been watching my obsession all those years.

I didn't have a clue about what to do about armpit wrinkles but Tracy began getting information on the subject on the internet after her fitting. She read, (goodness is this trait inherited?), that if you put Preparation H under your armpits, it would tighten the skin and the wrinkles would seem to disappear!

Tracy's Wedding
Ken Sklute/www.KenSklute.com.

Amazing!! And the best part is that you not only have wrinkle-free skin, but you also won't have that itchy, burning feeling from the discomfort of hemorrhoids there either!

I told her to "go with it" and we both learned something new! She tried it, it worked and she put that on her "Wedding To-Do List". Tracy looked absolutely beautiful in her gown on her wedding day and not an armpit wrinkle in sight! I added this valuable tip to my dressing routine at the wedding and every time I wore a sleeveless dress after that. I guess you are never too old to learn!

My brother once told me, "You are just afraid of getting old." "No I'm not afraid of getting old, but do I have to *look* bad while I'm doing it?" was all I said.

My daughters have been much smarter than I ever since their teens-just ask them-and it is not in their nature to surrender that perception. I proudly remember wearing a sweat shirt that said,

"Ask your Children while they still know everything!"

Not long ago, my daughter was watching me put on my makeup. As I was looking into my magnifying mirror applying eyeliner, she criticized me for putting on too much eyeliner. I was using liquid eyeliner since I had to give up eyeliner pencil a few years earlier as it would drag across my no-longer moist eyelids and *"stutter"* every time the pencil hit a wrinkle. I informed her that I had to put a lot on and then wipe the excess off with a wet cotton swab so it would "fill in all the wrinkles." "Someday you will see!" The thought was repulsive to her. She left the bathroom and left me alone with my wrinkles and my smart ass answers.

A very dear girlfriend of mine, a few years younger than me, recently asked me, "What do you do about the wrinkles on your neck?" Like God made me older than her just so she could get first-hand advice? In spite of the insult, I told her to apply plenty of moisturizer in an upward motion, rubbing from the bottom of your neck to your chin, while your head is facing the ceiling. "Do this every night." I said. "Mornings too." But then I added, "or after a while, the wrinkles just grow on you, (no pun intended!) and you just get used to them." In other words, "*Live with it!*"

AGE SPOTS

I never had freckles—well maybe a beauty mark here and there in all the right places! I again attribute this to my German heritage. I think one of my German ancestors got a little too close to the French border for some hanky-panky, and that's where I got the dark hair and healthy olive skin. I rarely burned in the sun and instead of minimizing the sun's effects with tanning lotion; I soaked my skin in baby oil before going out into the sun to "sizzle" and never burned.

At about the age of 48, I started getting "freckles" on my arms. That was okay with me. They added some "character" to my body. I can live with that! It wasn't until my sister at the ripe old age of 49 came to visit me for a few weeks, that I found out I was deluding my vanity. She looked at my hands and arms and yelled excitedly, "You've got them too! You've got them too!"

"Got what?" I asked.

"You have age spots too, just like mine! See?!" as she showed me the "age spots" on *her* arms and hands. "These aren't age spots on *my* arms, they're *freckles*" I defended myself. "*Freckles my butt! They're Age Spots!*" she laughed.

CRATERS

At the age of 55, I was in the bathroom scrutinizing myself in the mirror and what do I see? "Craters" just above my right elbow. "What the heck is *that* now?" I asked myself. I turned and lordie, lordie, I had one on my left elbow too. A matched set! This new discovery made me stand upright, move closer to the mirror and examine both craters. "How gross!" Where did these come from?

So here are the facts, girls: This must surely be the "gravity factor" and it applies to more than the moon. Even though I try to work with my weights on a regular basis and swim three times a week, the skin on your arms apparently no longer has enough elasticity to stay where it belongs! As Newton with his apple as evidence would say, *"Earth's gravity pulls inward toward the center of the Earth's core",* which is down! Since we are upright creatures, and since the center of the Earth is down, the skin on my elbows is trying to find my wrists! Since bones have more density than skin, skin wins the gravity race, won't let the bones stop it and it droops in circles around the joints! Thus Craters! These half moon-shaped craters form on the outside of each arm beside the elbow. So I will never be able to wear short sleeves again and here we are, living in Phoenix where long sleeves are outlawed between June and September!

Gravity is most likely the reason for the wrinkles *above* the knees too. I am visualizing moon-shaped craters forming around each side of my knees as the wrinkles grow into layers and subsequently "unhappy faces" with moon craters as dimples are created. No more shorts or bathing suits after that! I will never be able to look at myself naked in the mirror anymore either! Just like all my other aging dilemmas, this too passes and I still wear shorts. Heat and discomfort always win out.

My maternal Grandmother, Lillie May, had such character-inside and out. She was quite spunky for her generation. She was strong and independent and had energy that wouldn't cease. She smoked cigarettes, swore when she wanted to, told grandpa what to do…and he would do it as he turned down his hearing aid so he couldn't hear her yelling at him, cleaned houses-*her* way-for other people, and was the drill sergeant for her twelve grandchildren. We all adored her and would fight for "our turn" to stay at grandma's house for the weekend. Each one of us grandchildren had our own crochet hook, (even the boys!), and we would sit in a circle making chains of yarn for entertainment. She would draw pictures on an old pillow case, give us an embroidery hoop and needle, and teach us how to embroider. She was a pro at Parcheesi but I *know* she cheated and she would never think of "letting" someone win. She called all of us "her brats" and would threaten us with our lives if we were stupid enough to cross her. She was definitely "*the boss*" and we all loved that woman!

After grandpa passed away and she was in a nursing home, I chose her as one of my subjects for a photography assignment. I shot black and white film, some in natural light, some in flash. I finally chose two photos to matt and frame. One with a smile; one with a more "distant" look. I exposed the film and processed both photos with high contrast paper. Living as hard as grandma did-smoking, many hours of sunlight and never really taking the time to take good care of her skin, her face was full of wrinkles and lines at the age of 83. The high contrast development intensified the wrinkles. These are among my favorite photos of her.

Hartenfeld Family Album Photographer, Barbara Hartenfeld circa 1983

When I showed grandma the framed and matted photos, she looked at them earnestly and said, "Where did all those wrinkles come from?" I told her, "I love every one of those wrinkles, grandma!" And she smiled. One day as I was looking at my own "crow's feet" and some new lines around my mouth, I thought, "My goodness, I'm starting to look like Grandma Hyde!" I looked deeper into my eyes in the mirror, squinted as usual to see just how many wrinkles really were there, and said to myself, "I loved that old woman *and* her wrinkles. *Maybe this won't be so bad after all!*" If I have anyone at all that loves me as much as I loved my grandma-wrinkles and all-I will be a blessed woman.

So you see girls, aging can't be all that bad. Wrinkles define your personality and can be a roadmap of the life you have lived. It's your soul that shines through your eyes that are framed by all those wrinkles that reveals your true spirit. The soul never changes even if your face does. Look into my soul through my eyes as I get older. The wrinkles only frame the wisdom I have earned through the years. As you look into my face, you will also see all the love I have given and had returned by my wonderful daughters.

CHAPTER SIX

The Eyes Have It

Hand drawing. Artist, Barbara Hartenfeld

When I was about nine years old, I kept getting headaches so my mother took me to see Dr. Walker, probably the only eye doctor in town. He didn't want to put me into glasses just yet so he prescribed "eye exercises" and some nasty eye drops that burned when you put them in your eyes. I have absolutely no idea what the purpose of all this was, but I reluctantly did my "eye exercises" daily-for a little while at least.

I had to go into my bedroom twice a day after mom put the eye drops in, turn the lights out and put these dark glasses on to read the special book he gave me. I was to read and point at objects. This part was really hard to understand. My mother left me alone in the room and closed the door, so if no one else was in the room with me, who would know if I touched the right object? Maybe my mother was supposed to do these exercises with me, but how would she find the time with three little babies to take care of?

After about three days of this routine, I got a little bored. The third day, I read only half the book. The fourth day, it was just a few pages. Since I didn't want my mother to know I wasn't doing my exercises, I had to find other things to do to occupy my time in the dark bedroom so she wouldn't find out. On about the fifth day, I read one or two pages and then began fooling around with my nose. It was convenient.

I would plug my nostrils and then try to blow in and blow out. Blow in and blow out. I guess I overdid it and with one hard blow, (either in or out, I can't remember!), I started losing consciousness. The already dark room got even darker, I began feeling light-headed, and I struggled to get to the door. With the last few breaths I had, I screamed for my mother!

"I can't see. I can't see! I'm going blind!"

"What did you *do?*" she screamed. "Rolly, get up here! She's going blind!"

"Oh boy, I really did it this time!" I thought to myself.

After all the excitement, I finally calmed down, (no help from my hysterical mother), and my eyesight returned. I thought that would be the end of it and I was darned if I was going to tell her I was playing with my nose instead of doing my eye exercises. But oh, no! She had a better idea!

"You're going to a specialist! I can't have you going blind!" she cried, still hysterical. The next week, I was on my way to a specialist in Cleveland, getting my eyes tested. "Just a little astigmatism", the doctor said. "I will prescribe a pair of glasses for her. They will be ready in a week or two." "No, Mrs. Hartenfeld, she is *not* going blind!" he added.

GLASSES! "Oh, my gawd! I'm still a little kid! I can't wear glasses! I'll never be the prettiest girl in the fourth grade anymore if I have to wear glasses!" I said to myself. "I will get laughed at! No one else in school has glasses!" All this because I was playing with my nose. Oh, well, at least I didn't have to do those stupid eye exercises anymore!

After that little "exercise" in futility, I was sure I was destined to go blind sooner or later, so I practiced being blind by tying a scarf around my eyes to see if I could find my way around the house. I gave that up after several bruised shins and scraped-up knees. Besides, I would practice being blind all by myself and that got to be pretty lonely and boring, so I just went outside and played with my brothers and sisters and cousins instead. That was much more fun. I may as well enjoy my eyesight as long as I have it!

Several weeks later, I was driving back from Cleveland with my dad and wearing my new white-rimmed glasses. As we were driving through a neighborhood, my dad said, "I'll bet you a dollar you can't hit one of those trash cans with this paper cup as we drive by, with those new glasses on!"

I would do anything for a dollar! I aimed very carefully and believe it or not, the paper cup slam-dunked right into the trash can sitting alongside the curb. Well, at least that's what my dad said. We were going much too fast in the car to tell. He gave me a dollar. Maybe this won't be so bad after all. At least I had a dollar!

From then on, I spent half my lifetime looking for my glasses. I was just too vain to keep them on my face all the time and then I would forget where I laid them down. See girls, this has been going on for long time. Getting old has absolutely nothing to do with it! One time I ran to my dad to tell him my brother stepped on my glasses and broke them. For sure my brother would get blamed for this one and I wouldn't get yelled at this time. Instead, dad said, "So Butch was walking on the table again?" knowing quite well I had probably left them on the floor just like the last time!

I have had to tolerate glasses since I was ten years old. I tried contact lenses but I was allergic to all the solutions. They hadn't invented soft lenses yet! I decided I would only wear glasses when I had to see! I would never be caught dead in them for a photo! *I hated wearing glasses!!*

My eyesight started getting worse when I was about 35 years old. I had just graduated from college and gotten a job as an estimator for a folding carton company. I had no idea what a real estimator did when I started, but one of the responsibilities was to sit all day in front of a computer. Computer screens were really hard on your eyesight then. You know, all those x-rays and gamma rays that come shooting out from them all day long. Before long, I needed to wear glasses nearly all the time and I had to get stronger prescriptions. The eye doctor explained that it wasn't just the computer, "After all, you *are* over 35!" *Gaud!* Did he really have to remind me? When I was 35, 35 seemed middle-aged and I really didn't need someone reminding me! I'd rather be playing with my nose!!

At about the age of 43, the eye doctor decided I need bifocals. *Bifocals? Me? Why me?* Gratefully, they had invented graduated lenses by then. The doctor stopped me from beating the floor with my fists and just before I jumped out a second-story window by telling me about this wonderful discovery. He showed me a sample copy of the graduated lenses with no line and I agreed I would be able to do this. *Bifocals-43. Bifocals-43. Bifocals-43.* Hard pill to swallow. I was numb!

What I didn't know until years later is that graduated lenses are actually <u>trifocal</u> lenses. One for distance; one for normal; and one for close-up. Let's see, I was over 60 by then and all this time I thought I was wearing bifocals. Sometimes ignorance really is Bliss! It worked for me for fifteen years, until I was ready for the truth!

To this day, I still don't like my glasses but I wear them all the time now, because I'm sure I would be legally blind if I didn't. The reality that forced me into making this ground-breaking decision came when I had gone into a grocery store without them. You know-the vanity thing again. I had to stop doing that when I could no longer read small print on bottles and had to ask for assistance from the cashier to use the debit machine. "Can you help me out? I left my glasses in the car." The cashier laughed. What's so darn funny? Wait until *she* gets older!

As I said, my ego has somehow survived and I wear my glasses all the time now. As you age, they tell me, because of depleting moisture in every part of your body-including your eyeballs-things start to dry out. There is an additional, more scientific bit of information too. From lack of moisture, your eyeball forms into an oval shape instead of a round shape that allows 20/20 vision and that is what distorts your sight. How gross! I don't care what the reason is! I will always hate wearing glasses. Except of course, after a good cry. Then you can use your glasses to cover up the puffiness. *SEE!* (What a pun!) Glasses are good for something after all!

Today there are other solutions for vain people like me. Lasik surgery is one way. I've talked to people who have had it done with success and others that weren't quite as successful. Of those people who are my age, they either need to have one eye adjusted for close-up and one eye for distance and just need time to adjust. Sometimes, they never do. Others have both eyes adjusted for distance and still have to use "cheaters", (inexpensive magnifying glasses you buy at the drug store), to read. You have to be awake during Lasik surgery and if the process doesn't work the first time, you need to go through it wide awake again. I also have the thought that this process is so new, that there really aren't any long-term cases to convince me that this procedure really is permanent.

As for me…all of this seems like an awful lot of work! It's taken me this long to bite the bullet and wear my glasses all the time, so this is what I choose to do. I am a chicken when it comes to surgery wide awake with your eyes open!

And it just keeps getting better and better! Read on...

POSTMENOPAUSAL DRY EYE

Nope! I hadn't heard of it before either until of course, *after* menopause. According to an article I read, hormonal changes after menopause result in your eyes drying out due to a decrease in the activity of your tear ducts. (As if bifocals weren't bad enough!) This results in "chronic dry eye". This was actually good news! Before I read the article, I was sure this was the first stages of going blind. (There I go again!)

After menopause, I began having great difficulty reading even with my glasses on. My eyes burned and I couldn't focus after reading only a page or two of a book. My eyes were so tired I had to quit reading and take a nap instead. Not that I hadn't learned to appreciate a good nap more and more as I got older! I was never an avid reader, but there were books recommended by my friends that I really wanted to read and have you ever tried to read the tiny print on a prescription box or instructions in a new appliance manual? I tried getting stronger "cheaters" thinking it would relax my eyes so I could get a few more pages in or actually read the directions on a label! When that didn't work, I tried using my "cheaters" plus a super-powered magnifying glass but got tired of moving the magnifying glass over the sentences- side to side to side to side-*and* I couldn't always find the magnifying glass anyway.

Arizona is famous for its *"dry heat"*-that's how we are able to tolerate the 110 plus degree summers-but this was getting ridiculous! During allergy season, the beginning of our *"dry heat"* season, I used a lot of

"AC" eye drops—you know, for itchy, watery, allergy eyes, and my vision got *worse-not better!* Nothing seemed to work! It was easier just to quit reading! That is until one day when I grabbed a bottle of ear drops from my medicine cabinet by mistake, (because I couldn't read the label!), and instead of the eye drops, I put *ear drops* in my eyes! *Burned like Hell!* The bottles, through my post menopausal eyes, *looked* the same! Who am I kidding? At least I didn't grab the wart removal bottle sitting on the same shelf! The drug companies thankfully had the common sense to make *those* bottles in a different shape! *Wow!* Can you imagine what *that* would have felt like?

So while I was frantically rinsing the ear drops out of my eye with cold water, it hit me! "Itchy, watery, allergy eyes…" Key word—*watery!* My eyes weren't watery at all. *They were dry!* Time for some research— before I actually do go blind from using too many ear drops in my eyes!

The result? I didn't have allergies at all. I had…you got it… Postmenopausal Dry Eye! At least that's what the article I read said- once I could read again when my eyes healed from the ear wax remover! The article also included a coupon for ultra, high-performance, over-the-counter eye *lubricant* for Postmenopausal eye dryness! The first time I put the drops into my eyes was like having a crystal clear water fall running over them! What relief!

I went to my eye doctor not long after that and took the eye lubricant drops with me. He told me that was the best choice I could make before getting prescription-strength eye drops. He also told me that I could use them as many times a day as I needed them. I began with five to six times a day and was able to taper off after the first week. The drops helped immensely but I wanted even more. I had an ice pack in the freezer so I started applying that, but again, I seemed to be taking a step backward. I finally realized that my eyes didn't need to be cooled, they needed moisture! I applied a wet wash cloth on them once a day for moisture and then saw a commercial for salads with cucumbers. A light went on and I went straight to my local supermarket and purchased a cucumber. Now I put a cucumber slice over each eye and *then* the moist wash cloth. Double dose of the wet stuff!

Learn something new every day and that's just one of the many reasons why I am writing this book-so you don't waste time and money on useless remedies for chronic post-menopausal dry-eye and more importantly, don't accidentally put ear drops in your eyes like I did! See how much time...and agony I am saving you?

Another piece of valuable advice—I rearranged my medicine cabinet so I keep all eye products and ear products, oh, and wart removal on different shelves. Can't be too careful!

A word to the wise: You only get one pair of eyes! Take good care of them or, (are you ready for this?)...you'll go blind!!

CHAPTER SEVEN

"I would give my eye teeth for that..."

Before I had my first daughter at the age of 23, I had perfect teeth. My teeth were white, straight, and I didn't have a cavity or a filling in my mouth. Five months into my pregnancy, I had eight cavities that had to be removed and filled. My dentist explained that the baby was draining the calcium from my body and considering the rate my teeth were decaying, I expected Tracy to be born with a full set of teeth!

After having my second daughter three-and-a-half years later, my cavities were so deep that I began having abscesses which resulted in root canals and crowns. I had my first root canal and crown at the age of 31. Since then I have had 14 root canals and 19 crowns done by dentists all over the country and Mexico. I can tell you which teeth were done and in which locale. My first crown was done in Ohio. Seven crowns were done at one time across the front of my mouth in Connecticut. Three root canals with crowns were done in California only to be replaced in Arizona, where I had an additional three more root canals. I had five more crowns done in Algadones, Mexico. Thank the Lord for dental insurance and discounted Mexican dentists! After all that, I had invested over $40,000 into my mouth. That would be a nice down payment on a house!

What all the dentists failed to tell me is that the crowns have a time-destruct mechanism installed in the porcelain, and that they only last ten to twelve years. *Then, you get to have them done all over again!*

Another natural phenomenon of aging is "receding gums". I wasn't aware of this biological indicator until I started seeing the shiny metal tops of my crowns peeking out from my gum line! "Can't you just fill in the crown back to the gum line?" I asked my Arizona dentist? "Oh, no. You need to have the crowns replaced" was her reply. Cha-ching! Another $40,000? In *this* mouth? *No way!*

So here I was at "that stage of life" that I need to decide whether or not I should keep my teeth, or should I say "crowns", or wake up to my teeth in a jar next to my bed every morning for the rest of my life? What a horrible thought!

I told that dentist I would think about it but never went back. I had to think. Metal gums with money in the bank, or get new crowns. There *had* to be a better way out of this! I went home that day with my complimentary tooth brush, dental floss and travel-size toothpaste but more importantly, at the suggestion of that dentist, I invested in an electric tooth brush. (So why did she give me a free manual tooth brush?) The electric tooth brush has stimulated my gums enough that they are growing back down to my teeth and the crevices between my crowns and my gums are barely noticeable. This only delays the inevitable, but I have a little "breather" before having to make another major financial decision. This is also the reason everyone in my family got electric tooth brushes for Christmas that year!

Years later, my crowns and natural teeth began to crack with time and even with the help of the electric tooth brush, my gums were still receding. I knew I needed to get some dental work done. Of course, my dentist convinced me that it is always best to keep your teeth whenever possible. *My* teeth? By now they were 80% manufactured!

After a complete dental exam, and this time with no dental insurance, I found out I needed to invest another $8,600 here in the states. The same work cost only $1,800 in Mexico so I endured three hours driving each way over a period of four months and my teeth were once again presentable. What I didn't know was that it is more economical getting my dental work done in Mexico for a reason! Three years later, the Mexican crowns began falling out while my made in the USA crowns are still holding up after nearly twenty years! So I was once again facing the decision to brush and floss or keep my dentures in a jar next to my bed overnight. Not a pretty picture, is it?

I finally went to another American dentist for them to help me make the decision, "keep the teeth" or "pull the darn things and get dentures!" The first dentist wouldn't even look at me if all I wanted was to pull my teeth and get dentures. The second dentist finally understood that getting dentures was only one option. I needed good advice from a "woman of my age", to make a good decision.

Here are a few pointers on why you should keep your natural teeth as long as you can.

1. When you remove the bottom teeth in particular and replace them with dentures, the jaw bone begins to deteriorate.
   a. Stage 1. You have to continually go back to the dentist to have your dentures realigned because of the deteriorating jawbone.
   b. Stage 2. You are forced to start using denture powder or denture cream to make your dentures stick to your gums and I am guessing it leaves a nasty after-taste in your mouth. (This sounds more and more disgusting all the time!)
   c. Stage 3. Your facial features begin to change as your jawbone shrinks. Picture *that* one! Your chin and jaw can now droop

down into the rolls of your neck so your face and neck look like a roller coaster starting from your lower lip down to the turtle neck sweater you are now forced to wear every day for the rest of your life. Doesn't sound very pretty, does it?

2. After they scared the living daylights out of me and I decided to keep my teeth, the first procedure I needed to have done was to remove the stump of a tooth left from my Mexican crown that fell off. I'd had six other teeth pulled before so that didn't frighten me at all. Stupid me! After pulling, tugging and prying for 20 minutes, the dentist pulled out the big guns...*the drill!* "The root of the tooth has masticized onto the jawbone. We are going to have to cut it away," she said calmly. "Is that okay with you?" Okay with *me?*

Point number one-my mouth was stuffed with bloody gauze and I could not communicate other than shaking my head for "yes" or "no". She couldn't understand a word I said! My mouth was full of carbocane, my tongue was certainly three times its size, and besides the fistful of gauze in my mouth I had a steal "squirty" thing hanging out of it!

Point number two-I'd already lost a pint of blood and I was on my third dose of carbocane. Did she really think I would stop her *now? "Just get it done and get me out of here!"* I just shook my head 'yes'. I guess she had to ask!

She drilled the tooth away from the jawbone, impacted me with yet more gauze and gave me a week's supply of pain killers and told me to come back in the morning so she could see how I was doing. "In the morning?" That showed real confidence. She must have thought my family would sue her if I bled to death during the night! After feeling the hole the extraction left, I asked her if I shouldn't have a prescription for an antibiotic because of the crater she left in my gums. "Oh, the hole's not *that* big!" she said. "It just feels big right now. It will be okay once the swelling goes down." *I believed her!* Big mistake! Three days later, I have infected gums. The infection spread throughout my lower gums, then to my sinuses and my glands. I was miserable! I was better off with the Mexican stump.*! Give me drugs! Give me antibiotics!*

Once the soreness in my mouth diminished to the point I could stick a finger in my mouth and pull the lip away so I could see her handy work, I was shocked at the hole in front of my gums! *I have been mutilated!*

After a few miserable days racked with pain and infection, I went back to the dentist and asked her to explain all this. She gave me the name of a paradontist who could build up the "hole" in my once-healthy gum with...get this...gum grafts, before they connected a new bridge using the surprisingly healthy teeth left on either side of my "crater" to bring me a new $3,500 smile from three teeth that no one can see even when I smile!

So this is the *real* point of # 2: If this is what happens when they pulled just one tooth-I can't imagine what would happen to me if I had all my lower teeth pulled! "NO" to dentures! Keep your natural teeth as long as you can no matter how nasty they look!

It took me a couple of years to go back to yet another dentist when I was experiencing another abscess. Another Mexican crown fell off. I was sure they would just pull it but again, they insisted I "try to keep my own teeth". $1,300 later, I had a new crown but swore I would never go back to that dentist either. Of course there is a story involved!

I had to get my teeth cleaned and all new x-rays taken. When the dental assistant was rinsing my mouth with the "squirty thing", she missed my mouth and hosed down my foot! "Oh, I am so sorry," she said. "Me too," I thought. "Where's the door?" They decided they could save the tooth since it wasn't abscessed after all, so they cleaned it out and prepared for a new crown. "Come back in a week after it heals", she told me.

The next week, anxious to get a new crown, I was sitting in the chair next to Miss Water Hoser who was taking measurements and trying to fit the new crown. She poked and prodded and kept asking, "Does that hurt? Does that hurt?" Even if it did, I wasn't going to tell her. I've been to this rodeo before. I knew if it hurt, that indicated a root canal was necessary and I wasn't about to go through another one of those! "It *will* hurt if you keep poking around like that!" I told her.

New crown; new debt. I walked through those doors knowing I would never be back. Another dentist "bites" the dust. Well, it wasn't over yet! The Mexican crowns started pulling away from my gums one at a time. Time for some serious dental decisions. I needed another consultation and someone to give me good advice so I could figure out how I was going to pay for this. Life is so unpleasant when you don't have dental insurance.

Yet another new dentist, (of course), new location, new opinions. This time I told them due to my age and family history, I could no longer consider saving my teeth. Upon x-rays, I was told that I actually had no real teeth on the top and only five on the bottom. How depressing! All that previous dental work and this is what I have to show for it! They gave me an estimate of having all of the top and most of the bottom teeth pulled and replaced with a full denture on the top and a bridge on the bottom so I could avoid the deteriorating jaw bone syndrome. $5,050 and I would have to go ten days without any teeth so the swelling could go down until the new dentures and bridges could be put in place! Having the work done didn't bother me but even though I have good credit and was approved for the loan, I was still uncertain as to how I was going to squeeze another monthly payment out of my already strained budget. I scheduled the appointment to pull the teeth for the end of October and would figure out the financial logistics later. Go for it!

Wouldn't you know it, my gall bladder had to be removed and that trauma sucked me dry of all my bravery and good intentions. I cancelled the extraction appointment and to this date, haven't rescheduled it. Doesn't look like anything will be done for a while. The saga continues!

Both you girls got braces after I found out that I wouldn't have had this much trouble with my teeth if I had had my teeth straightened with braces when I was younger. Apparently, if the teeth aren't aligned, they wear down, which leads to decay which leads to cavities, which leads to fillings, which lead to root canals, which leads to crowns, which all lead to your grandmother's dentures sitting on your bedside table! Probably *my* dentures too!

This all adds up to a huge investment which I would much rather have spent on a vacation home in Acapulco! To date, I have over $45,000 invested in my mouth and I still can't laugh out loud without covering my mouth with my hand! See what you have to look forward to?

And don't forget to floss!

CHAPTER EIGHT

Menopause

Do you know what the *real* spelling of "menopause" is?

MEN-A-PAUSE

This is the time of life when women feel so awful from night sweats, bloating, hot flashes, memory loss and irritableness from lack of estrogen that we become...*Queen Bitches! So*...men take "a pause" from us! Therefore, men-a-pause. I truly believe this proper spelling and description should be listed in Webster's!

This is also the time men start looking, (if they haven't already), for those sweet young things with firm breasts, tight butts, vivacious personalities, no brains, PMS, (which have similar symptoms to menopause but is much more forgiving to a 50-year-old male), and a minimum of two young children they want someone else besides their natural fathers with no money, to raise.

In this openly immodest age of advertising, we have numerous actresses, with unlimited budgets for plastic surgery, praising how "wonderful" each and every change of life stage a woman passes through is:

"Make up that hides wrinkles. Look years younger!" Baloney! On *her*, even wrinkles would look good. Ever notice advertisers use models that are in their twenties to demonstrate how well their product "fights the war against aging"?

Another from a lovely 30-something blond actress-*"A hair color: that actually covers the grey"*…as if she had any—and what man would notice if she had any? I'll bet no one knows what color her eyes are either!

Glamorous sixty-year-old movie star about denture adhesives and cleansers: *"Never worry about what you eat…don't give up the foods you like most…"* Can you imagine any of *them* sleeping next to a night stand with a cup of teeth floating in effervescent bubbles in a glass?

On the subject of HRT (Hormone Replacement Therapy): *"I went to my doctor and he prescribed HRT. As a result I have never felt better in my life!"* That's a lot of crap!

Do you ever wonder why there aren't any famous male stars advertising *Penal Failure?* Can you imagine Burt Reynolds, Michael Jordan or Joe Namath, (even though Joe did like panty hose at one time), advertising penis pumps, penal injections, or "Testosterone Erection Replacement Therapy (TER)? I just made that up but don't you think it's a good idea? Women are just too honest! For a buck anyway!

Those of us "typically" menopausal women just aren't that enthusiastic about our "changes". *Our* conversations go something like this…*"Damn!* There's another one! These hot flashes are a bitch and you never know when they'll hit!" as we wipe the sweat off our brow with a napkin. Or "…and he wants me to be all romantic in the morning when all I want to do is put some dry clothes on."

Now I hear the HRT (Hormone Replacement Therapy) I am taking causes breast cancer. Oh, great!

Men *love* making cracks about our biological stages. When we are in our twenties and thirties we hear, "Oh, she must be on the rag" or

"PMS—again? *I thought that was* <u>*last*</u> *week*", or "*I probably won't get "any"* *this week-it's that time of the month again.* "After forty-five, we hear, "Oh it's just "the change". She'll get over it in ten or twelve years if I can take it that long!" If *he* can take it that long? *What about US?*

As I said earlier, my dad blamed everything on "the change" whenever things weren't as comfortable as he would like it at home. He always relished being the hero and swore that my mother went through "the change" for twenty years. He thought it was rather funny. I wonder how *he* would feel having his first hot flash or waking up to soaking wet sheets. As far as being *"pissy"*, did anyone ever think that the reason women were so emotional during these years is that they had to put up with their male partners going through self-denial about the male mid-life crises they were going through?

Since having a hysterectomy at the ripe old age of thirty-something, I wasn't at all sure when the "change" would happen to me. The surgeons left one ovary and that precious little organ kept estrogen pumping through my veins for over 25 years all by itself. It did a wonderful job, too. Everyone tells me I look years younger than I really am and I'm sure it has something to do with the little bugger. I didn't have periods after the hysterectomy since the surgery took my uterus and believe me; I didn't mind that at all! I didn't like them in the first place and never missed them at all!

Neither I, nor the doctors, could really tell when menopause began for me. I went in for a physical shortly after my fiftieth birthday and even the doctor had to ask me, "How old are you?"

I just turned fifty," smiling because I knew I didn't look fifty!

"When was your last period?" he continued. Duffus! He didn't look at my files! "Twenty-nine years ago." I answered with an "I-can't-believe-you-said-that" look on my face.

"Oh, yes…you had a hysterectomy." (Light bulb goes on!) "I think it's time we put you on hormone replacement. You *must* be going through menopause by now. Do you have any symptoms?"

"What kind of symptoms are you talking about?" I was being a smart-ass.

"You know, hot flashes, irritability, rapid weight gain, loss of bone mass, vaginal dryness, decline in your sex drive…you know." No! I *didn't* know! And from the sounds of it, I didn't want this menopause thing anymore than I wanted the period thing when I was fifteen years old! The Alpha and the Omega of the female reproductive cycle. Who needs any of it? "Nope, none of them." I said proudly.

"Well, I think we should put you on hormone replacement anyway. I'm sure it's time!" Great philosopher this one was! "Let's see. You will need a breast exam, a colonoscopy, blood work, blood pressure evaluation, *uterine exam*…" I looked at him over the rims of my glasses. "Oh, yes…no uterus! Guess we'll forget that one." May as well, *he* forgot! "Ok." He continued, "I'll schedule the exams. We'll need all these tests before we can find the right hormone replacement therapy. We want to make sure you're healthy enough so you don't have a stroke or anything once you start taking it."

Good Grief! Now a stroke? What else?

I had all the tests, some not too pleasant, and I proved to be in "excellent health for a woman of *my age.*" (Isn't that such a comforting statement?) Somehow I knew I was going to start hating that phrase. The nurse told me, "You have the bones of a 35 year old woman!" Leave it to another woman to pay you a compliment that you can really appreciate!

So I started taking the prescribed medication in spite of the health warning put out by the American Cancer Society. After about three days, I started feeling "queasy" in the morning. A few days later, I was bloated, had full-blown morning sickness and my breasts started hurting! *"Somehow, I just don't think this is right!"* I said to myself as I dialed the doctor's number. I gave him my symptoms and he asked, "Is there any chance you might be pregnant?" *Good grief!* He forgot my hysterectomy again!! "No, I am not pregnant! I'm just throwing up every morning!"

"Maybe we should run more tests." *Bull crap!* I threw the darn HRT down the toilet and started feeling better right away. It was like a major victory! At fifty, my remaining ovary was still active and I didn't have to worry about "the change" for a while yet! Life is good!

About a year later, I was planning a vacation with my "man du jour" and found myself getting irritable at the *smallest* things. I would blow the whole relationship if I went on vacation in that state. *This was my first sign of menopause.* Mark this down somewhere! *Bitchiness!*

I didn't have night sweats, bloating, hot flashes or memory loss, but I didn't want vaginal dryness to sneak up on me on the first vacation I'd taken with a man since my divorce fifteen years earlier, so I called the doctor…a new *woman* doctor…and asked her if I could try HRT again. She never *once* forgot that I had had a hysterectomy! When I told her my problems with the first attempt, she told me to take the pills at night so if they upset my stomach, it would happen while I was sleeping. Only a woman would know! (This is one of many reasons why I was glad I switched to a female doctor!)

I started taking the pills at night like she said a few weeks before the vacation with little or no side effects. I had a lovely ten-day vacation with no vaginal dryness, no bitchiness and most likely-no loss of bone density because we did a lot of walking in New York, Gettysburg and Washington, DC and my bones didn't creak or hurt!

My boyfriend and I broke up after the vacation anyway. I attribute it to *his* first stages of "male menopause" when he started hitting on those sweet young things with firm breasts, tight butts, vivacious personalities and no brains.

Successful Stage One of Menopause

The next "real" sign I had was a very oily face and zits like I had as a teenager. I could take a cloth, wipe the oil from my face several times a day and polish the furniture with the cloth at the end of the day. I didn't totally understand this as the onset of menopause until my good friend, Beth, who is only a few menopausal symptoms behind me told me, "I don't know what to do with my face! It's so oily and my face is breaking out like it did in high school!" Sound familiar? Ah-Ha! This is one last chance for Mother Nature to make you feel like a teenager again before she shut everything down. Now tell me, couldn't she think of other joyous episodes related to being a teenager to remind you of your youth instead of "pimples"? Does this have something to do with the apple thing again?

Due to the medication, I wasn't having any physical signs of menopause, but emotional side effects were creeping up on me when I wasn't looking. At the peak of my career, I got fed up with the company I was working for and walked into my boss's office one day and *quit my job*. Talk about cocky! I gave up a nearly six-figure income on "principle" and actually felt good about it. That would have never happened years earlier when job security ranked right there on top of my list with compulsive vanity-driven exercise, being a good mother and having a date on Saturday night!

I gave my oldest daughter away at her wedding. I tried red hair for a few weeks. I dated a "biker man" and became a "biker babe" leather and all. I re-shaped my eyebrows and my pubic area. I let my daughters tell me how to wear my hair and clothes. I quit the singles club I had been active in for five years and told everyone to go to hell. I bought four pair of cheaters because I was always losing my regular glasses and I could never find my car keys. I started digging through my purse looking for something yet forgetting what I was looking for once I got tired of digging in my purse-just like my grandmother used to. And I bought a brand new shiny black two-door V-6 Honda with black leather seats, black tinted windows, moon roof, and enough bells and whistles to make any car enthusiast (or twenty-year-old), envious. You know-the car of my dreams. In retrospect-I believe all of these were very apparent signs of *midlife crisis syndrome* that should be listed in all the medical manuals as (tadaa!) *Menopause.* BUT...I didn't have any hot flashes! Who would have guessed?

I didn't have medical insurance for about a year after I quit my job. My HRT prescription was still good for about six months but after that, my doctor wouldn't give me another prescription until I had another physical and breast exam. Oh, well! I can beat this menopause thing without pills! *Wrong again!* I finally began having mild hot flashes without the pills. Very slight at first. Just a little uncomfortable. Then they got worse and worse and worse until I erupted like a volcano! The hot flash started in my lower back and never gave me advance warning. The very first one—and I remember it well—was in the middle of a Physic Party I was having at home. The intense heat, (and it really *was* intense!), traveled up my back to my neck and head. I was perspiring across my forehead and my scalp, then the heat traveled down my arms, made a statement in the center of my stomach and traveled to my abdomen. *This is not fun!* Thank the Lord I was with my girlfriends so I didn't have to make up any excuses!

By the time that first episode was over, I could wipe the sweat from the back of my knees and come away with enough sweat to water my house plants. My scalp would get wet and ruin my hairstyle, and I would be exhausted. I could almost compare it to labor pains...not so much with the pain but with the duration and intensity. Biggest difference, hot flashes last longer than eight or nine hours of labor, but at least you don't have another baby to raise for the next eighteen years! A silver lining in *everything* if you give it half a chance!

Sleeplessness! I have always been able to sleep through anything, (except of course hearing the two of you coming into the house after curfew!). Even stress has always had a difficult time keeping me from sleeping. Menopause is the only demon that has disrupted my sleep patterns. In retrospect, though, sleeplessness from menopause is the biggest contributor to this book. It may never have been written without it!

At the age of 58, I finally got some hope from believe it or not, the assistance of a Urinary Tract Infection (UTI). I wound up in the emergency room in excruciating pain, ready to pass out. After numerous tests, one being a pelvic ultra sound, (now *that's* one experience you don't want to miss!), the physician's assistant came into my cubicle with, "Well I have some *good news* for you!" In the state of mind I was in, *anything* would be good news as long as it included relieving me of this horrible pain!

"Your remaining ovary is only about *this* big," as she crunched two fingers nearly together to form the size of a small pea. "And this is going to make me feel better *how?*" I asked. "Your remaining ovary is nearly gone and menopause for you, my dear, is almost over!"

Well, by golly, this really was good news! But give me some drugs for now, *thank you very much!*

I was elated for only a month or so and noticed along with the drying up of the ovary, new wrinkles began appearing around my mouth and eyes and "middle-age spread" became more and more of a reality. Oh, and by the way, Osteoporosis is more likely to occur after menopause as well. Definite downside.

So with the end of menopause, came the onset of "different" symptoms of aging! I just don't have hot flashes or night sweats. *Whoopty DO!*

I am sincerely hoping that by the time you girls are ready to experience menopause that medical science has learned to make this stage of your lives more comfortable without giving you cancer. That will happen as long as more *women* enter menopause prevention research. With so many females entering this specialized profession, I wish one of them would also discover a pill that would make men experience all the joys of menopause women have experienced since Eve—*even if only for a day*-so they can honestly relate to what women have had to endure and maybe, *maybe*… men will finally get off our backs!

How about that?

I found the following saga in an email and would like to share it with you. It sums up my feelings about the effects of middle age and menopause. I have no idea who the author is, but I would like to thank her! (I am certain it was a *her.*)

A.A.A.D.D

"They have finally found a diagnosis
for my condition. Hooray!!
I have recently been diagnosed with A.A.D.D.!
Age Activated Attention Deficit Disorder…
This is how it goes: I decide to wash
the car; I start toward the
Garage and notice the mail on the
table. Ok, I'm going to wash the
car. But first I'm going to go through the mail.

I lay the car keys down on the desk,
discard the junk mail and I
notice the trash can is full. Ok, I'll
just put the bills on my
desk and take the trash can out, but
since I'm going to be near
the mailbox anyway, I'll pay these few bills first.
Now, where is my checkbook? Oops,
there's only one check left. My
extra checks are in my desk. Oh,
there's the coke I was drinking.
I'm going to look for those checks.
But first I need to put my
coke further away from the computer,
or maybe I'll pop it into the
fridge to keep it cold for a while.
I head towards the kitchen and my
flowers catch my eye, they need
some water. I set the coke on the
counter and uh oh! There are my
glasses. I was looking for them all
morning! I'd better put them
on first.
I fill a container with water and
head for the flower pots—
Aaaaaagh! Someone left the TV remote
in the kitchen. We'll never
think to look in the kitchen tonight
when we want to watch

television so I'd better put it back in the
family room where it belongs.
I splash some water into the pots and
onto the floor, I throw the
remote onto a soft cushion on the sofa
and I head back down the
hall trying to figure out what it was I was going to do?
End of Day: The car isn't washed, the
bills are unpaid, the coke
is sitting on the kitchen counter, the
flowers are half watered,
the checkbook still only has one
check in it and I can't seem to
find my car keys! When I try to figure
out how come nothing got
done today, I'm baffled because I KNOW
I WAS BUSY ALL DAY LONG!!!
I realize this is a serious condition
and I'll get help, BUT FIRST
I think I'll check my e-mail..."

It helps to know that you are not the only one going through this. Misery really does like company! Feel any better, girls?

CHAPTER NINE

"You Said What?"

Self Portrait Photographer, Barbara Hartenfeld circa 1985

I went back to college when I was 33 years old. Unfulfilled as a cashier, stocker, dairy and produce assistant, and all-around grocery gal, I decided one day to "take this job and shove it!" I carpooled to school with a girl 15 years my junior who had a 1972, two-door Chevy Impala with typical Ohio rust eating at the exterior. The solid iron body of that relic wouldn't allow the rust to eat completely through and that frame created the strongest, heaviest doors imaginable.

The winds in March can be pretty ferocious in Ohio. One day after classes, I had my arms full of books, art portfolio over my shoulder and a few fingers left to grasp my art kit. It was difficult enough getting into the car in that wind, but all the items I was carrying made a make-shift sail. You know, like the Flying Nun's hat.

Ivy and I finally made it to the car. I wouldn't dare put anything down to open the door or it would blow away. Anything lose would be gone forever wrapped around an olive tree and off to Oz. Not wanting to lose any of my supplies, I took a remaining finger to open the heavy steel door of her car and slid my butt into the front seat of the car. Just then, a major gust of wind blew the car door shut. The force of the wind combined with the solid steel door created a vice with my head in the middle! It knocked me out *cold!* By the time Ivy got into the driver's side and realized what had happened, I was already coming to with a "deer-in-the-headlights" look on my face. "What happened?" she asked.

"Huh?"

"I said...*what happened?*"

I could see her lips move but nothing was coming out of them! I don't even think I cared! She pried my fingers off the supplies I had left in my arms, threw them into the back seat and kept staring at me, moving her lips again. I could tell it was something like "G Damn Car! Piece of Shit Car! G Damn car! Piece of Shit Car!"

Already my head was pounding and I couldn't hear <u>anything</u>! I tried to lay my head back onto the seat. My head seemed so heavy! Then, I put a hand on each side of my head and started rubbing my head. "*Ouch*" I screamed.

"What's the matter?" she yelled. Two large bumps, bigger than goose eggs but smaller than flying saucers, had already formed on my head! And they *hurt. My gaud*, they hurt! A few days later, after trying to resume a normal life, I finally admitted that I needed to see a doctor. I could hear a little better, but the ringing in my ears was incessant! Every time the microwave went off, piercing pain engulfed both ears. And every time I tried to read my homework, my eyes would jump up a line instead of going down to the next line. I was scared! After several tests, the doctor told me I had a concussion.

Concussion? He also told me that I had lost 25% of my hearing in my left ear and 45% of my hearing in my right ear. If I lost hearing, why did loud noises and alarms make my brains shake? Didn't make much sense to me at the time and still doesn't.

So, many years later, as the natural process of aging depletes your ability to hear a pin drop or your young children one story up whimper in the night, your lovely children say,

"Mom, you have GOT to get a hearing aid!"

I learned to lip read after my accident many years ago. I also learned to tune out the voices of my daughters as a natural defense against terminal whining! There have been many times that I have stood right in front of them listening to their latest sagas and I didn't hear a word they said. For example, one day, Tricia was telling me something I imagine was very important to her, and suddenly she looked at me and said, "Mom! You didn't hear a word I said, did you?"

"Nope." I said, and walked away!

Crowded places are the worst! Background noise interferes with sounds I *want* to hear. Still too vain for a hearing aid, I have adjusted to smiling like a Cheshire cat and nodding my head once in a while when someone is talking to me. This seems to work…I think. Or are my friends and family just being courteous and walking away saying under their breath, "Deaf as a Door! When will she get a hearing aid?"

My daughters have told me that some stores have free hearing tests. Finally, in tears, I gave this explanation: "First of all, I can't *afford* a hearing aid right now. The tests may be free, but the hearing aids are expensive-especially the small inconspicuous one I would like to have. (They didn't know that I had been investigating.) "Secondly, it's hard accepting the fact that I need one! I see little bits of my body getting older one piece at a time and I haven't convinced myself yet that I'm old enough to need a hearing aid. *"Just leave me alone!"* The subject hasn't come up since but I still hear them mumbling as they walk away, "Deaf as a Door! When will she get a hearing aid?" I will be forced to take care of it someday. Like Scarlett. "I'll think about it tomorrow!"

I did have some vindication one day just before my youngest daughter turned thirty-seven. SHE had to ask me to repeat something I had said very plainly. "I'm having trouble hearing voices in a busy room sometimes", she explained. *Oh! There IS a God!* And she didn't ever have her head caught it a car door either! Now, maybe she will get off my back about *my* hearing! I am so blessed to have lived long enough to experience this! So very, very grateful!

CHAPTER TEN

Exercise, Exercise, Exercise

Now I know you girls can run circles around me when it comes to keeping fit through exercise and weight training. Especially you, Tricia, You competed in professional body building and know everything there is to know about nutrition. But I think I have done some very positive things in my adult life to stay healthy and contribute to looking and feeling younger than my chronological years. Aside from the many pieces of exercise equipment and videos I have purchased (and later sold at garage sales), and numerous health club memberships through the years, I believe swimming laps is by far, the most result-producing exercise in my fight against aging.

In my early thirties-you know when I first noticed my butt was beginning to sag-I joined the local YMCA to help me keep what used to be my twenty-something figure. I signed up for two aerobics classes and a weight lifting class. I really enjoyed the aerobics and made some new friends. After several weeks of weight training, I felt pretty frisky and extremely indestructible. As I usually do, I asked a little more of my body than what it was capable of doing. While doing a set of reverse sit-ups, I felt a little ripple up the back of my right leg. I stopped for a moment. "What the hell was *that?*" I asked myself under my breath as I looked back at my leg. Nothing I guess.

So I went back to my reverse sit-ups until I heard an undeniable "pop" in the same leg. Then the pain set in. Instinct made me bend my knee and rub the back of my leg. "Maybe a Charlie horse," I said to myself as I continued to rub and knead the knot that was forming in my leg. Nothing seemed to help. The pain intensified. So typical of me, I looked around the room to see if anyone was watching me before I made my next move. I tried to get up off the bench and not only could I not stand on my leg, but even more pain shot through the back of my knee. I hobbled to the locker room and figured it would just go away, but I couldn't have been more wrong.

As days led into weeks, the pain worsened with each passing day and I finally had to go to the doctor. He told me I had torn my hamstrings. Funny, I didn't even know what a hamstring was! How can you have something on your body all these years and not even know what it does or what it's called, until it rips out of place?

The doctor put me in a leg brace, told me to ice it and to start therapy. "You can either ride a bicycle or swim", he told me. Well, when you live in the northeast in February and there's snow and slush on the ground, it doesn't take a rocket scientist to figure out that bicycling is out. So I started using the pool at the YMCA three times a week. I would take my leg brace off in the locker room, hold onto a wall and hobble and make my way to the pool. My first discovery was that *muscle injuries don't hurt in the water.* You can do anything you want in the water with little or no pain that on land, you cannot do.

Secondly, I found out that I really enjoyed swimming and this was the beginning of my passion for the water. After only a few weeks of this régime, I was able to tuck the brace away in a closet and begin walking again with very little limping. After two months, I forgot about the pain and was walking normally again. I continued swimming because it made me feel so doggone good, and I went back to weight training-only this time, I was a little wiser and actually knew now, why the instructor told me to warm up thoroughly before and after lifting.

Over the years, I had several other injuries in my quest for the perfect body. Most of them, well-*all* of them, were because I always asked too much of my body and when I least expected it, tore or pulled some other part of my body. Then I would head back to the pool-actually my fountain of youth with chlorine. In my forties, I started swimming on a regular basis, even when I didn't have an injury. I could exercise my entire body at one time and I couldn't rip, tear, or break *anything* while I was in the water.

Then came my fifties. I was still taking my body for granted and still expecting it to respond to every physical whim I had. I had just gotten back from a ski trip to Tahoe where I noticed my other leg starting to cramp up when I skied. I figured it was because I tensed up when I skied because skiing scared the hell out me, and my muscles were tightened. I applied ice, sat in a hot tub, rubbed and massaged my leg. I never imagined that this was the beginning stage of the worst leg injury of my life.

Two months later, I hiked Havasupi Canyon, near the Grand Canyon, with some friends. It was an eight mile hike down to an Indian reservation, over-night stay, and then another five mile hike down a cliff to Havasupi Falls. The sights were awesome; I overcame my fear of heights with some vertical climbing down a mountain; took some incredible pictures and overall had a wonderful time. That is, until we had to hike eight miles back up to the top. I wasn't at all prepared for this. As we neared the top of the canyon, the trail got steeper and was full of switchbacks. I thought my lungs were going to burst and my heart would beat right out of my chest! All those weeks of short hikes and going up and down stairs didn't seem to prepare me or my body for this kind of workout! I had to stop every fifty or sixty feet and rest on a rock.

"Look at that lady's face! I've never seen anyone's face so red!" a little girl said. I told everyone else to go ahead because I truly thought I would die before I reached the top. But I didn't die! I made it all the way to the top. My leg hurt a little, but after a few days on flat ground, I hardly noticed the pain or the limp I was developing. Always busy, busy, busy, I didn't give it another thought until one day when I was home alone and coloring my hair, (again!). I had a roommate, but she wasn't home, so instead of ruining another shirt with the hair color and since it was the middle of a Phoenix summer, I colored and timed my hair in the nude. Well, wouldn't you know it; I hear footsteps and then a key turn in the doorknob.

"Oh, my *gawd!*" My roommate was home and here I was sitting in the living room in the buff! My roommate was about twenty years younger than me and I couldn't imagine she would want to see me in my birthday suit and my stinky hair piled on top of my head with hair color! So I jumped out of my chair, hurriedly did a u-turn into the hallway that led to my bedroom and I heard another audible "Pop! Pop! Pop!" I fell to the floor in excruciating pain! Again, vanity dictating my behavior, I crawled to my bedroom, dragging my limp, lifeless, leg behind me, and closed the bedroom door just as she was coming in the front door.

"Whew! That was a close one!" I said to myself. And then the reality of the pain set in. I had never felt anything like this in my life! Immediately, my whole leg started swelling and turning black and blue. I hadn't hit it on anything. Why was it turning black and blue? I really didn't know what to do. As I sat on the bathroom floor biting into a towel to quell my screams, I could hear my roommate walking around in the apartment, but I didn't want to ask her for help because I was still naked. I *really* needed to rinse the color out of my hair-it was long overdue, but I didn't want to make any noise like screaming and crying or beating my fists against the floor-or she would come in and see me lying there naked! Oh, the damn vanity thing!

Finally, I heard her go back out the door. In my relief that she was gone, I didn't give a thought to the fact that I really did need help! I couldn't get up, the swelling was getting worse and my leg was turning blacker and bluer. "What on earth did I do *this* time?" I asked myself.

Somehow, I managed to crawl to the bathtub and rinsed the color from my hair. Not knowing what to do next, I wrapped my now enormous leg in a towel, and pulled my hair dryer off a wall hook down to the floor. I couldn't get up on my feet! There I sat, trying to style my hair, (vanity, vanity, vanity), on the floor and put on a little make-up. I knew I had to call someone soon for help but I sure wasn't going to let anyone see me without makeup and without my hair looking good! (This all sounds so absurd now looking back on it!) Oh! Getting dressed would be a good idea too! I was till naked.

By the time I started looking more like myself again, my leg was nearly double in size and was throbbing with pain. From the floor, I pulled the wall phone off the hook and started dialing for help. I called nine people and no one was home on this Sunday afternoon. "How am I going to get to the hospital?"

I lived on the third floor with no elevator and I could not come up with any great ideas on how I was going to get down to the car with this "dead weight leg" dragging behind me. Even if I got to the car, how would I drive myself to the hospital? Fortunately, sometime later, my daughter, Tracy, stopped by my apartment on her way home from Mexico. When she came in, the horror in her eyes when she saw my leg made me realize the seriousness of my injury. This was indeed, the *Mother Lode* of all injuries!

Right after that, my roommate walked in the door again. This time I was relieved to see her-I had clothes on this time! Between the two of them, they got me down the three flights of stairs on my butt, step-by-step, into my daughter's car and to the emergency room. Seeing my swollen, blackened leg, the emergency room attendants took me into an examining room right away. While waiting for the x-rays, I noticed the pain in my leg vanished. It really didn't hurt anymore. Now, I have had torn muscles and I have had pulled muscles and I was hoping I had just *pulled* the muscle. Since the pain had stopped, I was sure it was just a pull-not a tear. I kept saying to myself, *"Just a pull—not a tear! Just a pull—not a tear!"*

"The pain stopped because your leg is so swollen it has cut off all the nerve endings and you just can't feel it anymore", the doctor said. *Damn!* Please, please. *"Just a pull—not a tear!"* Unfortunately, not only had I torn my calf muscle away from my kneecap, but it had taken the Achilles muscle with it! When the calf muscle tore away, my leg started bleeding internally and that's where all the black and blue color was coming from. The only pink I had left was on my toes and that was fading quickly. At least I could still *see* my toes!

Well, I had really done it this time! My injury began skiing, was worsened by the hike and all I needed to do was twist it the wrong way in my nude escape from the living room to finish it off. Another leg brace, bandage wraps, crutches and physical therapy for six months!

Back to the pool. I swam laps every morning for weeks, even if it made me late for work. After two weeks of therapy, the doctor told me the swimming was better therapy than anything he could do for me, so physical therapy stopped-at least at the clinic. I continued swimming, and swimming, swimming until my leg healed

Since then, I have continued a regular swimming regiment. You can actually get addicted to this exercise. Not only does it keep your whole body tuned, but I meditate and pray while swimming. At the age of 59, I was swimming twenty laps three times a week. After having back and neck problems my whole life, swimming keeps all my muscles in tune which keep the bones in place and it also keeps my lungs clear and strong. All that water cleans out the sinuses too! Healthy or injured, I would recommend everyone hit the pool whenever they can.

REAL WATER WINGS

When you add aging with woman's other natural enemy-gravity, you get "water wings". You know-those cone-shaped extra terrestrials that grow under your arms that flap in the wind and jiggle when you raise your arms higher than a 45 degree angle away from your body. To make matters worse, you cannot press your arms tightly against your body or they separate and spread evenly to the sides of your arm to make your arms look twice their size.

There are a few things you can do about these atrocities that prevent you from going anywhere besides the shower without covering them up. In Phoenix, Arizona this is extremely difficult to do since sleeveless tops are mandatory ten months out of the year.

Warning One! One thing you should never do. Never, *ever* stand in front of a mirror naked, stretching your arms out to your sides, elbow bent and touch your hand to your head while using the opposite hand to see how much the water wings jiggle. This move is extremely depressing. Take my word for it, if you have come to his point, they *will* wiggle. Save yourself from the trauma and just get dressed in a top with sleeves in a dark closet.

Warning Two! Don't ever let anyone take a photograph of you while you are wearing a bathing suit, sleeveless shirt or a dress. This may damage your self-esteem and confidence permanently when you see the photo.

One option is to of course, exercise.

Step One: Hold both your arms out at a 90 degree angle and do ten small forward circular revolutions and ten backward revolutions. Pick up the revolutions as your arms get accustomed to this gravity fighting exercise. It doesn't seem like a lot but the water wings will fight you every inch of the way and your muscles *will* spasm if you don't work your way up to more repetitions slowly.

Step two: Still with both arms to the sides, move your hands back and forth from an upright position down to your shoulders-both arms at the same time. It will look like you are trying to flex your muscles even though there aren't really any muscles there yet. Begin with ten repetitions and "vision" the muscles for now.

Step three: Grab two 3-5 pound free weights. With your arms to your sides, elbows bent with the weights in your hands facing up, pull the weights up toward your shoulders and back down again. Do both arms at the same time and start with ten repetitions.

Again, with all these moves, work your way up to more repetitions and heavier weights. Do this for starters and work your way up slowly. There are hundreds of exercise and toning videos on the market. Find one that is just right for you. That is how I got started. Do them long enough and you can make up your own routines and exercise while watching TV.

And then there is my favorite way to fight "water wings"-in the water. Your arms pull your body through the water and get a great workout doing laps. You don't even have to think about it. Swimming

CHAPTER ELEVEN

What a Great Time to Live!

I once envied my grandparents for the segment of history they lived in. They were born between 1901 and 1905-the turn of the century. I would imagine they heard their parent's talking about the Civil War, slaves and Abraham Lincoln. Their grandparents were immigrants who most likely shared their stories of the "old country" and how they came to America.

Lucille and Ervin Hartenfeld
Hartenfeld Family Album circa 1917

May and Everett Hyde
Hyde Family Album circa 1921

I loved listening to their stories. They saw the first electric lights in houses and gas lights to light the streets and indoor plumbing. They cut wood for their kitchen stoves and had coal furnaces or space heaters to warm their houses in the winter. In the hot summers, they used hand fans and wet cloths to keep themselves cool. There were no air conditioners yet. They washed their clothes by hand and hung them out to dry on a clothes line. Milk was delivered in glass bottles by a milkman who drove a horse-drawn truck door-to-door.

They probably don't remember it themselves, but I am sure they heard their parents talk about the Wright Brothers and their first airplane flight in 1903. My great-great-grandfather, Owen Richardson, celebrated his 94th birthday in 1931 by taking his second ride in an airplane. His first flight was a year earlier. He died a year after his picture was in the local newspaper, a happy and fulfilled man. Owen was born in 1837 in Bloomington, Indiana. He never learned to read or write but he lived during the Civil War and the assassination of President Lincoln. Imagine everything he must have seen and experienced in his lifetime!

In 1908, Henry Ford invented the first automobile. It was called the Model T. Your Grandpa Barney had one that he renovated years later. It was a classic!

The unsinkable Titanic sank in 1912 and went to the bottom of the Atlantic Ocean. My grandparents were not even into their teens yet, but I am sure they heard their parents talking about it. World War I began in Europe in 1914 and the United States joined the war a few years later. That same year, the first traffic lights were installed in Cleveland, Ohio. The very first telephone was invented in 1915 by Alexander Graham Bell and the rotary dial came one year later. Can you imagine life without a telephone now?

1920 was a big year. Women won the right to vote. Until that time, only men had that privilege. Your great-grandmothers were in their early twenties when they voted for the first time.

Between 1923 and 1926, refrigerators and radios were invented! Until that time, my grandfather cut ice on Lake Erie in the winters and sold the ice to the city neighborhoods for their "ice boxes". He drove a street car for a living and when he was old enough, he used his experience as a street car conductor to become a railroad engineer. That is how he made a living for over 50 years.

The Great Depression started with the Stock Market Crash in 1929. My grandparents were in their late twenties and had small children by then. They saw bread lines and neighbors out of work and starving. Grandpa Hartenfeld took every run the railroad would offer him to keep his family fed. While he was on a run, Grandma Hartenfeld took in borders, washed and ironed their clothes and took in sewing. My grandparents were fortunate since they had already bought a house from your great-great grandmother for $3,000 and let her live with them in the two-bedroom home with three children until she passed away. In many ways, they didn't realize they were poor. Everyone was poor!

World War II, "The Big One", began on December 7, 1941 when Pearl Harbor was bombed. Your grandfather and great uncles all served in the war-some in the Navy, some in the Air Force and some in the Army. At one time, your great Uncle Ervin was presumed dead when his submarine, "The Jack", was missing in the Pacific Ocean for over six months, presumably sunk. He miraculously appeared on a street corner in Long Beach, California and bumped into your Grandpa Rol. What a reunion-just like you see in the movies!

Women began taking the place of the men in factories and on professional sports teams. This was their first taste of independence and the beginning of a new era for the little wife and mother at home. Many women didn't want to give up their jobs when the men returned.

World War II ended in 1945 after the Atomic Bomb was dropped on Hiroshima and Nagasaki, Japan. Albert Einstein regretted inventing the Atomic Bomb after he saw the devastation it caused. One crewman on the Enola Gay, Major Ferebee, had a nervous breakdown after the war. He was the bombardier who actually released the bomb that killed thousands upon thousands of Japanese citizens and it broke him. Little did they both know at the time that this horrific gift of death and destruction that killed and disfigured hundreds of thousands and their descendants throughout Southeast Asia during the war, that this would one day run ships and light up cities with nuclear power. The silver lining?

Although my grandparents witnessed so much in their lifetime, I had never taken the time until now to reflect on the marvelous things I have experienced in *my* lifetime. I want to share them with you and perhaps you will envy me as I did my grandparents.

I am a Baby Boomer. I was born in 1947.

In that same year, United States population was at 144,126,000. The average cost of a three-bedroom home was $6,640 and the average annual income was $3,031. A brand new Ford cost $1,086. A gallon of gas cost 23 cents per gallon. A loaf of bread cost 13 cents and a gallon of milk cost 78 cents. The Marshall Plan was established to provide massive aid to European countries to recover from World War II. Princess Elizabeth, heir to the throne in Great Britain, married Prince Phillip, The president of the United States was Harry Truman and there was no vice president. The New York Yankees beat the Brooklyn Dodgers in the World Series.

I didn't experience World War II first hand but I heard endless stories from my dad and uncles and saw movies about it years after it was over. John Wayne, superstar of the 1950's played many a war hero at countless World War II battles and he was my hero until I found out what a male chauvinist he was! Dwight D. Eisenhower, formerly known as "General Ike", was now president and living in the White House. The world was at peace and "the good life" was about to begin. My dad was honorably discharged from the Navy after the war with a medical disability that claimed he was sterile from contracting malaria in Panama during a tour of duty. "Sterile" as he was, he then proceeded to impregnate my mother five times-so much for the medical disability! I was the second child, only 15 months younger than my older sister. Mom and Dad weren't really ready for a second child so my dad drove mom in the car on bumpy roads and made her take hot baths and ran her through fields in the middle of the night to make her miscarry. They didn't have birth control pills yet and abortions were illegal. So on November 29, 1947, I entered the world.

When I was only two years old, the first Volkswagen Beetle Bug hit the highways. In 1950 the Korean War began. I don't remember much about that. I was too busy being a kid and no one really talked about it much. My Uncle Don served in the US Air Force but he was stationed in Germany. I lived out on a farm for a short time when I was little where I had kittens and I remember some of my toys. One special toy was a red fire engine car with peddles. My sister and I shared it. We shared everything.

Later, our family of five, moved into a government development called "MacArthur Park" dedicate to the memory of General Douglas MacArthur. The development was created to help our war heroes pick up their lives as a reward for their war service. There was a flagpole in the center of the development and every morning a veteran would hang the flag and salute. Patriotism was very popular then. My mother painted the linoleum kitchen floor black and then took a sponge and decorated it with red and white. They call it "faux painting" now. It was cheaper than getting a new linoleum floor.

By the time I was four years old, the very first credit card was used and *I Love Lucy* aired for the first time on public radio. We did all our dishes "by hand". No one had a dishwasher yet! My mother washed clothes in an "automatic" clothes washer. The first one I remember was electric, but it didn't have a "spin cycle". Mom put the wet clothes through two wooden spools called "wringers". One time, your Aunt Bonnie was helping my mother and she got her little arm caught in the wringer. By the time my mom got back down to the basement, Aunt Bonnie's arm was stuck half-way into the wringer. My mom pulled the electric plug and then screamed for my dad. They got Bonnie to the hospital. Miraculously, nothing was broken but Aunt Bonnie still has a scar on her arm from the accident. Mom was the first woman on the block to have an electric spin-dry washing machine because of this incident. Can you blame her?

There were no clothes dryers yet either. I used to help my mom hang the clothes on the clothes line with clothes pins. She kept them in a bag that hung on the clothes lines. I would hand them to her as she hung the sheets, towels and clothes out to dry. How I loved running through the clean fresh wind-filled sheets on the clothesline as they dried in the warm sun. When it was too cold outside, we would hang them in the basement where they dried by the heat from the leaky forced air furnace. Instead of "sunshine fresh", they smelled like a combination of musty mold and coal, but they were dry!

We had a game for the clothes pins. It was called "Drop the pin into the bottle". You see, since we had milk delivered to the house in those glass bottles, we had plenty and didn't have to go to Toys R Us! We usually returned the glass milk bottles to the milkman for a deposit, but mom would let us keep a few for the game. You would stand above the bottle and from waist-high, drop the clothespins into the opening. It had to be waist-high or everyone would yell that you were cheating! The person who got the most pins in the bottle won! This game was played at all birthday parties! It was a real hit! Right up there with "Pin the tail on the donkey". Most times, it was a hand drawn donkey and tails colored with crayons!

My dad always wanted to be the first one in the neighborhood to have everything, so we had one of the first black and white televisions. I remember having my mom turn it on and I would watch the test pattern until I got bored with it. Later I watched Howdy Doody, Captain Kangaroo, The Mickey Mouse Club, Sky King, The Lone Ranger, American Bandstand, Lassie, Ozzie and Harriet...and of course, I Love Lucy!

I remember Elvis Presley's appearance on the Ed Sullivan Show on our black and white television. My Grandma Hyde was at our house and mimicked the girls in the audience by falling off the edge of our chartreuse green couch onto the floor and screaming! Of course, that was long before she had arthritis and bad knees! I didn't know what all the fuss was about. You know this Rock and Roll stuff that my parents didn't like and wouldn't allow in our house. Must have been my dad's idea because years later I found out that my mom secretly had a crush on Elvis when I found a commemorative plate of Elvis hidden in the cupboard after she died!

We had a rotary dial telephone but the only thing you dialed was "O" for the Operator. She-and it was always a *"she"*-connected the number for you downtown on the main switchboard. We had a party line and if you picked the phone up quietly enough, you could hear your neighbors talking. We only needed three numbers and there weren't any area codes. *Can you imagine?* Somehow, I still remember my dad's work number. It was 622. That's it! Just 622!

In 1957, Henry Ford introduced the "Edsel" to the public. It turned out to be one of the biggest fiascos of the automotive industry!

In 1958, I was the Hula Hoop champion of my school. I even competed in some city-wide Hula Hoop contests. I would walk around in circles for hours and hours just spinning that darn Hula Hoop around my waist! No wonder I was so skinny!

This was about the same time that I had my first pizza too. At that time, an Italian friend of my mother's made pizza at her home. Later on, that friend's family opened one of the first Pizza Restaurants in Bellevue, Ohio. I thought it was a little weird being allowed to eat with my hands, but it really tasted good! This is how entrepreneurs were invented!

By 1959, Alaska and Hawaii became a part of the United States. I was in seventh grade and the history and geography teachers made a big deal of it! I guess history was being made right under my nose and I just didn't appreciate it! The Barbie Doll was invented that same year. I was certain she was named after me but of course, I was much too sophisticated to be playing with dolls anymore. I was into boys! But my little sister loved playing with Barbie, Ken and their friends for years.

In 1962, I sat in the living room with my dad and watched black and white television reports of John Glenn as he circled the earth in man's first orbit around the earth. Up until that time, the only proven things circling the earth were stars, planets, "Sputnik" and a monkey or two. I was a freshman in high school and I was now much more appreciative of the world around me. How amazing was this?

November 22, 1963 affected my life and the lives of all Americans. Aunt Bonnie and I finally got a television of our own in our bedroom and we would watch the news while we got ready for school. That morning I watched President John F. Kennedy and his beautiful wife, Jackie, board a plane in Washington, DC to campaign for the next presidential election. It was the first time Jackie joined the president since the death of their infant son, Patrick earlier that month. I went to school and in 5th period study hall; the principal announced on the PA system that our president had been shot in Dallas, Texas. "How could this happen?" I said to myself. I am sure that is what everyone else was thinking too.

In those days, we all respected our presidents-especially this president-so youthful and full of energy. His picture was placed in every room of the school next to the American Flag. We saw that picture every morning when our principal played the National Anthem on the PA speakers and we recited the Pledge of Allegiance to the Flag. (Yep! Even in high school!)

After that announcement, the silence in the study hall was deafening. We were all afraid to move. I think we all wanted to wake up from this bad dream and if we said anything at all, we wouldn't wake up-that the nightmare would go on.

The nightmare did go on. About half hour later, the principal announced that President John F. Kennedy died in Dallas from gunshot wounds to the head. I couldn't believe it! Still no one said anything. We just sat there with our books open, staring at each other waiting for the silence to break. Finally, I heard a girl crying, then two, then three. Students began leaving the study hall and I could hear more students in the hallways.

School was dismissed. All the buses were lined up outside the school to take us home because no one knew what to do if we all started crying! It was like a voiceless fire drill. We all walked to our busses automatically and still no one said anything.

The school bus was *never* this quiet! I am sure the poor bus driver was grateful that no one was talking or that he didn't have to help any of the students deal with this tragedy since I am certain he was trying to comprehend it himself.

I still had quite a distance to walk to my house once I got off the school bus at the end of my road. *Home.* Maybe I could get some comfort from my mom. I started walking and then running down the road and crying. Then I ran faster until I reached the solitude of my house. The president was shot! I ran to my mom and I could tell that she had been crying too. I couldn't even hug her. I just kept crying and hiding my face with my hands. I ran to my bedroom and turned the television on. "Maybe this was all a joke…a sick, sick joke," I hoped. But there in my bedroom, all by myself, I watched in horror as I saw the president's body loaded onto Air Force One in Dallas.

"It was true. It really happened. Our president is dead." I finally admitted to myself.

I watched Jackie Kennedy standing next to Lyndon Baines Johnson, while he took the oath of office. She still had the president's blood on her suit and she looked so tired. After the ceremony on Air Force One, secret service men helped her get back to the cargo area where the casket was placed and where she stayed during the long flight back to Washington, DC.

Bobby Kennedy met her at the airport and helped her off the plane and into a waiting limo. I remember being really mad that the limo door she was trying to get into was locked and she had to get help. "Who's the idiot who wasn't prepared for the president's widow?" I still wonder. She still had his blood on her suit.

School was cancelled the next day and then we had the weekend to be glued to our television sets. I turned it on the first minute I woke up and I stayed glued there except to get something to eat and go to the bathroom. I don't think I got dressed all weekend. I stayed in bed watching news reports constantly. I didn't want to miss any of this history.

On live national television, we all watched Lee Harvey Oswald shot down and killed by Jack Ruby in the basement of the jail he had been kept in. My family and I just screamed and looked at each other, barely believing what we had just witnessed!

Everyone in the country watched the president lie in state in the Rotunda. Devastated people, black, white, yellow, American, French, Canadian, European, young and old, rich and poor alike, passed by his casket for hours and hours. As I was watching, the color guard and secret service men escorted Jackie and little Caroline to the flag-draped casket. Jackie leaned down and made the sign of the cross. She whispered something to young Caroline and Caroline dropped to one knee and with a little white-gloved hand, she reached under the flag to touch the casket-I think-to get closer to her daddy whom everyone said was in that shiny box.

Everyone got strength from Mrs. Kennedy. We watched her march down the streets of our capital and we watched her comforting family members and heads of state with her grace. We watched her with her children. We watched little John-John salute his father's casket. We watched her lay a kiss on the casket at the gravesite before she lit the Eternal Light at the head of his grave. Later we watched her walk away to start a new life without the president.

I believe I want to share all these details of this American tragedy with my daughters so they can envision me living this very traumatic, very life-changing event in history. I remember helping them study their American History in fifth grade. As I helped them study the Kennedy days, I realized, my daughters only think of this as a small part of "history" that they will have to remember for a test. I *lived* it. It was not history. It was a very vivid, life changing memory.

I would imagine this is how my parents felt about World War II and my grandparents felt about World War I as they oversaw my own American History studies in high school. For the very first time, I had a new respect for the times my parents and grandparents lived in. This also made me realize that every person and event I read about from the past, were real people and events that changed and shaped *their* lives.

1963 was the year "The Beatles" invaded America! What excitement! I remember hearing *"She loves you, yeh, yeh, yeh…"* on the car radio and thought to myself, "How stupid is *that?*" But the more I heard it, the more I liked it. Soon all my friends and classmates were singing it while walking down the hallways. Then another song came out, and another and another. Paul McCartney was the dreamiest. Ringo Starr was absolutely cool and crazy. John Lennon was the witty one, and George Harrison was the quiet one.

Their first American appearance was on The Ed Sullivan Show. (Just like Elvis!) Mr. Sullivan introduced them by saying, *"and here are the Beatles!"* My gawd! The audience was going absolutely mad! No one could hear them singing. You could only hear girls screaming, crying and see them fainting all over the place. This was *"Beatlemania"* at its best. I loved it and my parents hated it! I still loved Elvis, Johnny Mathis, Frankie and Annette, Gene Pitney, Frank Sinatra, the Beach Boys and Fabian, but the Beatles were *sensational.* Just like Elvis, the Beatles changed Rock and Roll forever!

We heard rumors of the Viet Nam war in 1964, but hadn't quite been affected by it. I was a junior in High School. I was a Varsity Cheerleader, on Student Council, the junior homecoming attendant, president of the Art Club, dated the captain of whichever sport was in season, worked as a part-time cashier, teased my hair and sprayed it with extra-hold aerosol hairspray until it couldn't move. I put my make up on when I got to school and washed it off before I went home so my mother wouldn't know. With a little ingenuity I made sure I was one of the very first girls who wore a mini-skirt to school by rolling my skirt up and tucking it under my blouse or sweater. I was also one of the first girls to get sent home from school to change because my skirt was too short. After that, I had to drop to my knees in front of the principal to make sure my skirts touched the floor to pass his intrusive short skirt inspection.

Oh, yes, I was much too preoccupied to think about a war half-way around the world. But then, in the summer of 1964, a friend of mine joined the Air Force and was sent to Viet Nam. This definitely caught my attention! I got letters from Curt that made Vietnam all too real for me. He never went into detail but I could tell he was doing what he needed to do. I sensed that he had "changed" and that he was scared. Was the man who wrote these letters the same high school boy I knew? I answered his letters to give him a much needed jolt of the old home town. Even though we had never dated, he sent me an Air Force necklace in the shape of a heart with his picture in it. I think every service man there felt like he needed a "girl back home". I also think he was afraid he would never get out of Viet Nam alive.

Curt gratefully did get back to Ohio but another dear friend of mine, Herman Gant, didn't. Herman and I were good friends all through High School. He was only one of two black boys in our white high school and was also one of the most outstanding athletes Margaretta High School ever had! Herman Gant, Number 44, had such a splendid future in front of him. And he was my friend.

After graduation, Herman enrolled at the University of Toledo and was studying to become a social worker when he decided to "do his patriotic duty" by joining the Army. He stopped by the grocery store I was working at the night before he shipped out to say good-bye. I wished him luck, told him he had better come back alive and to make sure he wrote me. He said he was going to be a medic in Viet Nam and that he should be relatively safe. "I will write and let you know what's happening!" were his last words to me.

I never got a letter. Just a few months after he left, my mother got a phone call from Herman's mother. Herman Gant, a US Army medic, died of gunshot wounds while attending soldiers in a field in Viet Nam. His mother wanted me to know that he had three pictures of me in his wallet when he died and that she was so grateful that we were always such good friends.

A year later, my new husband left for Viet Nam for his third tour of duty with the Navy just five months after our wedding. While he was in Viet Nam I lived with my parents. Each day I would walk down our road to the mail boxes, praying for a letter from my husband who was off the coast of Viet Nam on an aircraft carrier. Seeing me walk to the mail box each day, one of our neighbors yelled out to me, "I hope he doesn't get killed!" So did I.

My two cousins joined the Air Force. One went to Thailand. One went to Saigon and each day my cousin in Saigon saw one less pilot or one less crew member fail to return to the barracks at the end of the day.

How real was Viet Nam to me now? Curt, Herman, my husband, my cousins and countless other brave young men and women across the country brought Viet Nam to my doorstep. It took a long time for our country to honor those who died for our freedom in Viet Nam. The Vietnam Veterans Memorial Fund was established in 1979.

Back to *my* history lesson!

I had graduated from high school, finished my first year of college on campus at Ohio University and had just signed up for classes at Bowling Green University extension courses that were held at Sandusky

High School for my second year. Firelands Community College hadn't been built yet so back to high school it was. At least I wouldn't have to drive and hour each way to get to the main campus.

Starting my second year of college and working full time I was 19 years old and bought my first car-a 1957 Chevy! That's right! I-your mother, owned one of the all-time classics. Well it was a classic for my generation anyway. Instead of the two-door I really wanted, I had a four-door and it had an automatic transmission instead of four-on-the floor, but I finally had my own car. I think it cost $250.00 plus tax and title.

Ten years on salted winter roads in Ohio is rough on any car. My car was no exception! It needed body work and a new paint job and the muffler was a bit noisy, but it was all mine and I had a *plan!* After a couple of years helping my brother-in-law keep his 1957 Thunderbird clean and shiny so I could earn 50 cents a week, I decided I knew enough about cars to bond-o the holes and sand and prime the car to prepare it for a new paint job myself. I asked a lot of questions at a body shop and bought the supplies. For weeks and weeks I filled the holes in the body from years of mid-western snow and salt and sanded and primed my car.

My dad had the bright idea that his cousin knew how to paint cars so I talked with "Uncle Ben" about the supplies I would need and how much he would charge for painting my already primed car. The one thing dear old Uncle Ben *didn't* tell me is that he had never painted a car with metallic paint and of course, it was silver blue metallic paint that I dreamed about!

I saved up the money, bought the paint and turned my project over to Uncle Ben. He looked very professional with his coveralls, face mask and paint gun equipment. Filled with excitement I waited in the house for the unveiling and kept peeking into the garage to see how the painting was progressing. I had to go to work before it was finished, so I didn't see the final project until I got home from work later that night. All I could think about was the masterpiece waiting for me at home! Since it was dark by the time I got home, I couldn't get a good look at it and I wasn't allowed to touch it, so I went to bed, anxious for the morning light. I rushed downstairs at the first signs of daylight to revel in the glory of my 'brand new" 1957 Chevy. I threw open the garage door and…there it was! My heart sank! The metallic paint had run in layers down the sides of my car! *"Dad! Come quick! Look at my car!"* I screamed.

Dad didn't come out of the house the first time I yelled but he finally came out the door and wasn't excited at all. *How can he do that when I am in the middle of a crisis?* Of course dad wasn't excited. Uncle Ben showed him my car before he left the night before and apologetically told my dad that he had never worked with metallic paint before and *"he really didn't know what to do with it!"* Dad knew how long it took me to save up the money and prepare the body. Cousin or no cousin, my dad threw him off our property! He nearly threw our sledge hammer, "Old Betsy", at him when he asked my dad when he was going to get paid! I don't think my poor dad slept at all knowing he was going to have to face me in the morning. And I thought *I* had a sleepless night. Dad had an even harder time facing me and giving me the bad news.

Since I didn't have any more money for new paint and didn't know who would paint it for me on my budget, I had to leave my car the way it was. *Oh, the horror!* I made the best of it, though, and it did get me back and forth to school and work. One day at work, I heard a customer make a remark about my poor car sitting in the parking lot as he looked at it through the store window, *"Boy! What kids won't do to their cars these days! That car looks like a blue cloud!"* he joked. He thought my car was painted that way intentionally!

So I christened my 1957 Chevy, "*The Blue Cloud*", put a black rubber ball on the top of the tire jack and placed it on the floor next to the driver's seat so from the outside, it looked like a four speed-on-the-floor transmission and proudly "buzzed the Ave". I guess you can survive *anything* with a little imagination!

Robert Kennedy and Martin Luther King were assassinated in 1968. I watched both tragedies unfold on the television in my bedroom. I couldn't believe this was happening again! There were race riots and marches on Washington. Young men all over the country were burning draft cards and American flags and moving to Canada in protest of the Viet Nam war. When will this be over?

Sitting in the living room with my dad in 1969, we watched Neil Armstrong walk on the moon on our new *color* television. I looked over at my dad as he sat on the edge of the couch in disbelief with his elbows on his knees and his hands holding up his head. He kept staring at the TV. I watched his face as Neil Armstrong said, "*One small step for man, one giant leap for mankind.*" I saw a tear come out of my dad's eye. We didn't say anything to each other. We just watched in amazement! A new frontier had just been penetrated!

1969 was also the year of "Woodstock" in New York and the year "Sesame Street" aired on public television.

Anti-war demonstrations and riots created headlines in 1970. Four students were killed by National Guardsmen at Kent State University. A friend of mine was a junior at Kent State. She was on The Green and witnessed the shootings. Her parents drove down there immediately and brought her home until things settled down on the campus. She was scared. We were all scared. What was happening to our world?

While this was happening, the World Trade Center opened its doors to the world and became the tallest buildings in New York and the United States. Little did I know then, that I would eventually see those two Twin Towers fall in my lifetime on September 11, 2001.

In 1971, eighteen-year-olds got the right to vote. Up until that time, you had to be twenty-one. My younger sister, Lori Anne turned 18 that year. Her whole class went down and registered together. They were a little disillusioned though. They were old enough to vote and go to war, but they were too young to drink legally! I don't really think that stopped them, though!

In 1972, NIKE shoes were on the market for the first time. I wish I would have known more about them! I could have made a million and here's how. Long before Nike came onto the scene, I always encouraged my daughters to shoot for the stars. Nothing was impossible. My words of advice must have sunk in because years later, my oldest daughter called me over to a table to talk with one of her classmates. She said, "Mom, tell him what you always tell us when we can't decide what to do about an important decision." So I told him. "You don't want to be 85 years old, look back on your life and wonder' what if'…so I always say, *"JUST DO IT!" Sound familiar?* Too bad I wasn't working for NIKE's Marketing Department at the time!

Richard Nixon was the first American President to resign after an unprecedented Watergate cover-up fiasco. *"I am not a crook!"* he said.

In 1974, the first VHS video recorder was sold. In 1977, Macintosh released the Apple II home computer. One year later, the first "test tube baby" was born in Great Britain.

Ronald Reagan was elected president. Thirteen months later, a gunman attempted to take his life as he entered the presidential limo. While he was in office he fought for freedom in Western Europe. He was persistent in demanding, *"Mr. Gorbachev, tear down this wall!"* until it finally happened in 1989.

Post-em Notes were accidentally invented that same year by a chemist who was trying to make permanent glue. CNN went on the air for the first time. So much was happening technologically and socially, that we needed a 24-hour news program to keep up!

Acute Immune Deficiency, (AIDS) was identified in 1981 after thousands of people had already died from this disease formerly called, 'The Gay Plague"

In 1983 Compact Disks were created and so was the Cabbage Patch Doll.

The American Space Shuttle Challenger exploded 73 seconds after lift-off from Kennedy Space Center in 1986. Seven crew members, including a school teacher from Massachusetts were killed. This event would change space exploration forever.

The Berlin Wall was finally opened in 1989 and was completely torn down by 1990. This ended twenty-one years of the "Cold War" which represented communism, oppression and the separation of eastern and western Germany. Communism was faltering and the Communist Russian government fell with it.

So now, my dear daughters, we have already entered your own history. These are the years you will explain to your children as *your* memories while they will call them "history" as they study this time in *their own* history books.

Let's see how old this makes YOU feel!

Don't worry! It happens to the best of us!

CHAPTER TWELVE

Please Treat Me Gently

Now in my sixth decade, I have added Senior Caregiver to my already full resume. My daughter, Tracy, saw an ad in the newspaper for "Caregiver-No license required." I was caring and giving and I didn't have a license, so it seemed to fit and I applied. Those wonderful grandparents of mine, two generations ahead of me always had so many interesting stories to share about a time in history I will never know and they always appreciated the time I spent with them. I never tired of their company as I went through my teens and into young adulthood. I spent hours and hours playing cards and games, taking walks, going on picnics, ice fishing, skipping stones on the lake, and talking with them. My most treasured and most valuable moments with them though, were listening to them talking about other times and places. I never grew tired of hearing their stories and now with Caregiving, I could have other elderly people to enjoy and to learn from. I never walked away from an assignment without learning something new.

I cared for a 100-year-old woman with a gentle spirit but with a tiger will if you crossed her or underestimated her capabilities. She slept a lot, but she didn't miss a thing! My job was to help her get to the bathroom on her walker while her 82 year-old-son ran errands and hung out with the boys and went flying. She stubbornly tried her best to sneak out of her chair onto her walker and start walking to the bathroom without me. She really couldn't understand why she needed a baby sitter and resented me being there at first. After a while, though, we found more things to talk about and we became friends. We both loved to sew and loved our families. We were a lot alike. She was just older.

I had two Parkinson's patients so I learned a lot about Parkinson's disease at the meetings and therapy sessions I took them to. My dear uncle was a victim of Parkinson's, so these experiences helped me understand the symptoms of his disease and what it was doing to him. One of my ladies with Parkinson's disease sang in a Parkinson's Choir and I took her to practice. At 82, she decided to have electronic brain stimulation surgery to minimize the tremors and involuntary movements that are associated with advanced Parkinson's disease. How brave she was!! Even with her challenges, she was such a positive person. The day after her second surgery, she had me take her shopping. She was determined to go on a long vacation after she got better and she needed new clothes. She wore me out!

I took another lovely woman to Mexico twice to have her teeth fixed. She had two teeth extracted and a new bridge put in immediately after the extractions, yet she boldly stood in the hot sun with me, waiting to get over the border without complaining. The first thing she wanted to do once we got over the border was go to McDonald's! She ordered a chocolate milk shake but I had to take the straw away from her and give her a spoon. The Mexican dentist had forgotten to tell her she shouldn't use a straw after extractions for 24 hours or she would get a "dry socket".

In the three-hour car trip, we discovered that we both loved listening to Dean Martin and I introduced her to IL Divo. She played some lovely Spanish music for me on the CD player in the car and sang along with the tunes. She also gave me Spanish lessons.

Willien Family Album
Photographer, Beth Willien Fakrieh
circa 2007

I cared for two elderly parents of one of my closest friends. Bob and Janet were 90 and 89 years old respectively. They were able to live independently when I first started taking care of them when Bob could no longer drive. They needed assistance getting to medical doctors, labs, eye doctors, dentists, x-rays, to the beauty shop, the bank and do some light grocery shopping. I spent most of my time with Bob while Janet was having her hair or nails done and what a wealth of information he shared with me. He confided in me because I'm not in a position to be judgmental like his daughters have earned the right to be. I was the friend that he lost years ago to a rest home or a disease or death. Bob didn't feel incapacitated when he was with me. He had a lot of wisdom and stories to share-so like my own grandfather-and he loved sharing them with an avid listener. He loved a new audience! We made each other laugh and shared secrets. He told me I was his best friend.

For a time, Bob and Janet lived with their grandson and his wife, who were their full-time caregivers. They were the lucky ones! So many elderly people live in nursing homes without family or visitors. Bob and Janet lived in their grandson's home and had the joy of their two-year-old great-grandson living there with them. I still took them to appointments and sat with them when their grandchildren wanted a night out. Later on, they moved in with their daughter. Janet had Alzheimer's disease. I sometimes wonder why her daughters still had her hair and nails done. Before Janet passed the beautician came to the house for her beauty treatment. Toward the end, she didn't have talkative days about years gone by any more. She had such an amazing life as a wife, teacher and mother of three daughters. Those days were memories at this point; memories for her and her family. Her anger, a symptom of Alzheimer's, finally left and she was too weak to try to pinch me anymore. When I first met her, she was such a very gentle lady. Now she just slept a lot. When she woke up from one of her naps, she would ask, "Where's Bob?" and once I assured her that he was not far away, she would go back to sleep.

After over sixty years of marriage, she and her husband no longer slept together in the same bed because Bob's arms were bruised from her pinching him all night. He missed her closeness as he remembered her the way she was and was saddened by the way she is now.

I would like to share a story about Alzheimer's disease with you.

I heard a story once about a young man asking his grandfather why he visits his Alzheimer-stricken grandmother every day. His grandfather didn't drive any more, but he got up every day, cleaned up, ate breakfast alone and then walked to the nursing home where she lived. He would take her for walks or comb her hair like he used to, read to her and wait for her to respond to their "conversations". But she didn't know who he was any more and she never answered. "Why do you keep coming if she doesn't remember you anymore?" the grandson asked.

"Because I remember who she is," was his loving answer.

Bob and I had a long talk one day. He wanted to talk about her disease. She was down to 68 pounds and slept most of the time. She would wake up for only a few moments and say, "I think I will lie down for a while," and then went back to sleep.

He asked me, "What do I do if I wake up in the morning, and she has passed through the night?" "You hold her one last time, tell her how much you have loved her all those years and how grateful you are to have had her in your life." I suggested. "Then go get Nancy. She will know what to do."

He asked me the questions he was afraid to ask his daughters. Maybe he knew they were too uncomfortable with his questions, or maybe they gave him all the right answers and he forget ten minutes later.

Over time, Bob developed congestive heart disease, had a pacemaker, and developed malignant tumors on both his kidneys. Hospice was assigned to take care of him and Janet both since their conditions would not improve. I don't know about other states, but the people of Arizona Hospice of the Valley are truly angels on earth. They come daily to bathe their patients, brush their teeth, dress them and make their beds. Periodically, they come to clean their living quarters, do laundry, and a nurse comes in on a regular basis to monitor their health.

I had taken Bob for a pacemaker check-up with his doctor. As we pulled into the driveway of his daughter's house, he said, "Let's not go in yet. I need to talk." So I parked the car and said what I always said to him, "What's on your heart, Bob? What are you thinking?"

"You know I have cancer, don't you?" he began.

"Yes I do Bob. Are you in any pain?"

"No," he answered. "I don't have any pain at all." He told me once that pain was his only fear of death and was grateful for not having any in spite of all the conditions he had.

"We *all* know you have cancer and we all pray that you don't have a lot of pain with it. We've talked about this before and we all know we are going to die sometime. The best thing you can do is to have faith in God, accept your disease and die as gracefully as you can. You know that all of us will be around you to support you and make you as comfortable as possible. Are you afraid to die, Bob?" I asked him.

"No. I'm not afraid to die, but I'm worried about what will happen to Janet." They had been married for over 64 years and he had always taken care of her.

"Bob, the same people who have been taking care of both of you will be here to take care of Janet when you are not here. You know that. Janet is in the best of hands and if that is keeping you from crossing over, it shouldn't be. You should feel free to move on to a better life in Paradise." Bob and I had had several talks about the peacefulness of death and the beginning of a whole new existence. He and Janet had had a long and blessed life together and he never wasted any time in his life-he lived it to its fullest.

"Is there anything else, Bob?" He had tears in his eyes. "You are my best friend, you know that, don't you?" he asked.

"Yes, I do Bob and you are my best friend too. I will be at your side every step of the way. Whenever you want to talk, we'll talk. That's what friends are for."

A week later, Bob unexpectedly had a massive stroke that affected his whole right side. His daughter, Beth, called me. She also told me that true to character, even after the stroke that left him unable to walk, Bob kept trying to get out of bed so he could talk to the other patients. As I said before, he loved having a new audience! They put a guard by his door and eventually put him in a lounge chair right by the nurse's station so they could keep an eye on him. Even in his weakening condition, he was always on a mission to make new friends! When I went to the hospital to visit him, he said, "When do I get to go home?"

I told him if he behaved himself and stayed in bed like he was supposed to, they may let him go home in a day or two. "What hotel am I in?" he asked. "Bob! You are *not* in a hotel, you are in the hospital. You had a stroke!" He looked at me quizzically and then by the astonished look on his face, I could tell that he finally "got it". He said, *"Oh, shit!"* I couldn't help but laugh!

He tried to tell me one of his stories and I had to ask him to talk more slowly, "I am having a hard time understanding you, Bob." So true to nature, he exaggerated the speed of his speech as if he was in slow motion, and we both laughed.

Bob passed away early on a Friday morning. His entire family was around him the whole week-and so was I. I learned so much from Bob. He was indeed my best friend and I was honored to be his. Janet passed away gently in her sleep a few months later. They were together again.

I took care of another couple. He was in a critical care facility with Dementia and she was in another limited care facility because she suffered from seizures and it wasn't healthy for her to be left alone. She is also the type of person who needs people around her. She gets lonely. Her body is incredibly healthy. I can barely keep up with her when she walks! This couple is so lovely-also married for nearly sixty years. What a full life they had! Travel, nice homes, socially active. Now they depended on their daughter, her friends and me, to drive one to the other's facilities to see each other. When I got them together, we went out to eat at some of their favorite restaurants or played yahtzee or rummy. There are so many moments that they feel "normal" but so many others that they feel sad and miss their old lives, they miss being together! He is the lucky one here. He doesn't realize he is living in a critical care facility.

For all of these wonderful people, I have become their best friend. I make them laugh and keep them busy. I give them someone they can talk to about their inner-most thoughts of sadness from missing their old lives. It's hard to share some of these thoughts with their children because the children think their parents are ungrateful for the care they so painstakingly chose for them. I look at pictures of the past with them and wait for a laugh but sometimes get tears instead.

Donald L. Hartenfeld
Hartenfeld Family Album. Photographer,
Barbara Hartenfeld circa 1990

One thing happens each time I see all of them. They hug me when I arrive and they hug me when I leave and say, "I love you."

I spent as much time as I could with my dear Uncle Don before he passed as his health declined from Neuropathy and Parkinson's disease. We have been close since I was a small child but toward the end of his life, we had some incredible conversations. One day, when his life partner was away, he coerced me into getting him outside by the pool. There were steps at every entrance to the pool from the house and he, being in a wheelchair, made it quite challenging to get him there. We had to be very creative and careful. If he fell, I didn't have the strength to get him back up into his wheel chair. I knew I would get into trouble for helping him, but he dearly loved the sunshine and warm breezes against his face. Somehow, we got him down the steps safely. He put his head back to feel the warmth of the sun and the gentle breeze on his face. "This feels so good!" he relished. Then he surprised me with this question. *"What does it feel like to die?"*

He knew I had studied near death experiences and reincarnation for years and he said he knew I was the only person he felt he could ask this question. So I did the best I could.

"Well, I haven't done it for a long time," I giggled. "But, I've read that you see a bright light and you are compelled to go toward it. Suddenly, you feel a big "Whoosh". As your spirit accelerates at great speed toward the inviting light, it leaves your tired and sick body. You have no fear, no pain." I continued, "You just want to go toward that warm, inviting light and then you see people that have passed before you, standing there with open arms, welcoming you into Paradise."

"What is it like when you get there?" he asked.

"I hear it's amazingly beautiful and peaceful. I understand that you are younger." I answered.

"*HOW* young?" he asked. "Oh, I think about 35." I made up.

"Oh, good! I really liked 35!" He brightened up.

We spent an hour or so by the pool until he was ready to go back into the house. I wouldn't dare let him out too much longer than that-he would get sun burned and then the cat would be out of the bag!!

On another afternoon, when we were alone, he asked me, "Why does God allow me to be so sick and have this dreadful disease? Why can't God make me better? I ask Him, but He doesn't answer my prayers." He was feeling very ill that day. Not even the foot, hand and leg massage I always gave him helped get him out of his melancholy state of mind brought on by the pain. So I told him, "Sometimes when God's children are sick and their bodies are so worn out, the only way to make them better, is by taking them to Heaven." He stared at me deeply with those incredible blue eyes of his for a short time and finally said, "I understand what you mean, honey girl. I am ready. I am not afraid." And we gave each other one long, incredible hug. It was one of the last hugs I got from him. He passed just five days later.

They talked. I listened. That's all they really needed. I needed to give them the most comforting words I could and I think I did. All these precious people helped me sneak a peek at the possibilities of my own future. I believe it is the unknown that frightens us the most. All the time I was their caregiver, they were really taking care of me.

Don't ever think a person near the end of their life doesn't want to ask questions and talk about dying. They do! Give them that opportunity if you think they might want to. Don't let your own uneasiness at the prospect of losing a loved one or a close friend thwart their efforts. They may be a little afraid and being able to talk about the true condition of their illness and discussing death gives them comfort and allows them to articulate their deepest inner thoughts. We all have that right. What you will be doing is giving them a precious gift.

Caregiving is by far, the most rewarding profession I have encountered. Spending as much time as I did with my uncle, my own grandparents, and my caregiver patients, I learned that every time you see an elderly person, look into their eyes. The eyes never change. You look past the silver hair, the wrinkles and age spots and if you look hard enough, if you care enough, you can see the younger version of them in their eyes. When you allow them to be young again in your own eyes, you give them the gift of immortality. It is then that they can share their thoughts and life dreams with you. It doesn't matter if they repeat themselves with the same stories time and again. It doesn't hurt to listen. It doesn't cost anything. Just Listen. It brings them joy!

I caught my own father looking into a mirror one day when he was just about my age now. I spied on him for some time from the hallway and then I finally asked him, "Dad, what are you looking at?" He hadn't seen me watching him and was startled. He thought he was all alone.

"I'm trying to figure out where that old man came from. I'm still the same person on the inside, but here's this old stranger staring back at me from this mirror. Where did all the time go?"

Well, now it's time for me to look into the mirror and ask the same question. All these experiences cumulatively have given me a lot of respect for our elderly generation because I *listen* to them. I look into their eyes and see that young person looking back at me through wrinkled eyes. These experiences have also helped me realize how I want to be treated when I am older. Here is a summation of my thoughts about entering the final stages of my life:

PLEASE TREAT ME GENTLY...

As I grow older, please treat me with dignity, with love and with understanding—no matter how hard I try your patience as you did mine when your hand was small enough to fit into my hand.

When I get older, please treat me with respect for I have seen things with my eyes that you can't imagine or may never see. I have experienced world changes that you only read about in history books. Yes, you have seen even more in your generation, but without the baby steps I witnessed, you would have never seen them at all. Through stories from my parents, I witnessed the pain, death and victory of a world war. I lost friends of my own in Viet Nam; watched children of friends of mine go off to senseless wars in the Middle East. I saw terrorists invade our country. I saw our own New York City Twin Towers destroyed. And I learned to pray every day for a world at peace—like God intended it to be.

Because of my years, I have loved more and longer than you have at this point. I have experienced more joy and more pain. I have seen more births and more deaths. I have experienced more victories and more defeats. I have seen more of God's wonders.

I experienced stay-at-home moms, closely-knit families and fun times without computers, i-pods and remote controls. Those lost times are now only warm memories that I wish I could share with you to teach you strong family values where love is measured by the time spent together instead of how many things we own.

I have seen people I love die too early because medical science didn't grow quickly enough to save them, yet that same pain drove men and women of my generation to research and discover more so your generation would not have to experience the same premature losses.

Before it's too late, ask me about myself when I was younger. What did I like to do, who were my friends, who was my first love, what class did I like best in school? What were my dreams? What dreams didn't come true? Get to know me as someone else besides your mother. Get to know me as your friend.

Ignore that tear in my eye when I pass over my driver's license to you because I have become a liability on the road due to failing eyesight or because of physical disadvantages. Beyond the tear and the wrinkles, see me at 16 when I passed my driver's license test, waiving that temporary license in the air, and running and jumping up and down toward my proud yet fearful, mother.

Don't whisper behind my back or put me in another room even if you don't think I can hear you or understand you. Try to include me in decisions about my life-where to live or how to divide up my possessions when it's time to sell the house because I can't afford it or can't take care of it any more. Through my eyes, try to see the excitement in my eyes as a young woman, signing the escrow papers on my very first house.

Put your arms around me if I look confused or lost, the way I held you when you were little, on a stormy night and you couldn't sleep. You don't have to say a word, just be there and hold me. I will have fears that need to be kissed away too.

Even if I am blind, share old picture albums with me when you see I miss my old friends or yearn for the family times together when you were little and you really needed me. Laugh with me when I laugh, cry with me when I cry over those lost times and we will lock those moments into our memories forever.

When you look at me when I am old and tired, and I am gazing into nowhere, know that I am wishing I could have one more swim in the pool, one more boat ride on the lake, one more hike up the mountain, hear one more cry of a brand new grandchild, go to one more school play, football game or dance recital, one more first kiss, one more laugh with friends, one more walk without limping, and one more dance. Mostly, just one more dance...

Please treat me gently, my dear children and your children will treat you gently as well.

CHAPTER THIRTEEN

Saying Goodbye

All of a sudden, I am *"The Next Generation"*. I am on the top of the heap now. Instead of just a Baby Boomer, I am a Senior Citizen Baby Boomer! Oh, where has the time gone?

As my grandparents got older, they soon became the only people left of their lifetime circle of friends. They still had their family of course, but one-by-one, their friends were dying. I asked Grandma one day, "How do you deal with all this, grandma?"

"With what?" she asked.

"You and Grandpa are either at the hospital or the funeral home. How do you deal with all this illness and death?" "Well," she told me, "when you get to be our age, you realize that death is just a part of life and we learn to accept it. When some of our friends get so sick, they actually welcome death. Grandpa and I will die someday too. Then it will be your turn to accept death for what it is-a part of life." The thought of them dying and leaving me sent chills down my spine! *My* grandma and grandpa? No way! She could tell what I was thinking-as usual. "Grandpa and I aren't going to live forever, you know!" That was over twenty years ago and here I am-the older generation and I finally understand what she was talking about.

While driving home from Bob's Memorial Service, I realized that death *has* become a part of my life now too. Spiritually, it is the best part. It is the beginning of your life in Paradise-your reward for a good life. Emotionally, it can leave you empty when you are the one left behind.

My cousin Judy passed away in January of 2011-the same day Bob died. Judy was only 66 years old. She was the first one our generation to pass.

One high school girlfriend died of cancer. Another died of heart disease. Another dear friend of fifty years has recently been diagnosed with lung cancer. Talking with my high school reunion committee I was told they weren't sure how many of us would be left for our fiftieth reunion in 2015. "We're dropping like flies," Billie told me.

So like Grandma, I accept death now as graciously as I can. Death can either get you down or you can accept it for what it is and draw energy and courage from those who have passed, to continue their legacies.

My granddaughter asked me once, "Mamaw, why do people die?" I told her it was God's plan to make room for new babies. That seemed to satisfy her five-year-old mind and in a way, it satisfies mine as well.

I have had to say goodbye to several friends and nearly all my family in the generation that came before me. I can't say you get "used to it"; I am just saying that you finally accept death as a part of life and that is not to be feared. Fortunately, I have a strong faith in knowing that life is just a layover between spiritual lives and that we all see each other again in the afterlife until we deserve the right to stay in Paradise with Jesus. I am a firm believer in Reincarnation and that souls close to us in this lifetime will be reunited with us again. We travel in packs and return lifetime after lifetime together, loving and learning from each other and growing wiser with each lifetime. Our time apart is only a fraction of the time we are actually together.

Death Be Not Proud

Death be not proud, though some have called thee
Mighty and dreadful, for, thou art not so,
For, those, whom thou think'st, thou dost overthrow,
Die not, poor death, nor yet canst thou kill me.
From rest and sleep, which but thy pictures be,
Much pleasure, then from thee, much more must flow,
And soonest our best men with thee doe go,
Rest of their bones, and souls deliver.
Thou art slave to Fate, Chance, kings, and desperate men,
And dost with poison, war, and sickness dwell,
And poppie, or charms can make us sleep as well,
And better then thy stroke; why swell'st thou then?
One short sleep past, we wake eternally,
And death shall be no more; death, thou shalt die.

By John Donne

CHAPTER FOURTEEN

Conclusion

They say that *"getting old has it rewards"*. I find that true in watching my children and grandchildren grow. There are some days I feel I could have done better in preparing my loved ones for life's realities, but there are also days that I know that I did the very best I could. As I got older and wiser, I also learned that I had to let go and let them "do it their way".

Me and My Girls
Glamour Shots circa 1998

My daughters are independent and courageous. My daughters are beautiful inside and out. My daughters and I have faced a lot of challenges, sometimes together, sometimes apart, but we have always persevered and when one of us was weak, the others made us strong.

There was an old German phrase on my dear grandmother's kitchen wall that read, *"Ve Get Too Soon Oldt and Too Late Schmart"* I see the truth in that old saying more clearly with each passing year.

"We are a product of our past". I have found that our growth escalates during troubled times. You have no idea how difficult it is to watch your children make mistakes and try not to interfere unless you have children yourself. I learned a long time ago that no matter what advice other people gave me, I still had to experience things myself, my own way, before I truly learned and grew from it. Remembering this, my dear daughters, you may not understand, but if there were ever times that you felt I wasn't there for you-I really was. Only I knew you had to make your own decisions and fall down if you had to, all by yourself. Life isn't easy. I was preparing you for the possibility of even harder times ahead. I cried when you weren't looking.

When you lose someone you love, you reflect on their life and how they touched your own. You try to hold onto them by remembering the impact, good or bad, they made on your life. Sometimes you are totally unaware of their influence on your life until one day you say, "My goodness, Uncle Don would have done that", or "my mother used to say that!"

Wrinkles and sagging butts are the *least* of your challenges when you get older! It's what happens to you inside that really alters you! While you are worrying about the tiny wrinkles around your eyes and your clothes don't fit you like before because of a sagging butt, other things are happening that kind of sneak up on you! You know-the things you can't see coming! Like, who would have ever imagined that you would someday have trouble walking because of a weak knee or an elbow that hurts when you try to throw a ball to your grandchildren?

Or that you would never again be able to read a book without glasses. Better yet, that you would have a hard time finding those glasses when you needed them!

Before you realize it, you can't run without worrying about breaking something, pulling a muscle or wetting your pants. You remember how effortlessly you ran as a child. Harsh reality but you can't avoid this natural process we call aging.

All of sudden you have a thyroid problem and have difficulty keeping the weight down when you could eat anything you wanted to when you were younger and never gain a pound. Aside of the thyroid, you begin growing a second butt in the front and no matter how many sit ups you do, it's still there.

You see your sisters, your brothers and your friends diagnosed with various ailments-lupus, fibromyalgia, arthritis, Parkinson's disease, prostrate disorders, carpel tunnel, have hysterectomies, get cancer … the list goes on and on. Your friends begin to consider retirement. You start learning to lip read because you are too self conscious to wear a hearing aid and all of a sudden you have a line of vitamins and prescriptions in a daily pill box on your counter like grandma and grandpa used to have.

During the different stages of life, you get one wedding invitation after another or attend baby showers because all your friends are getting married or having babies. You talk about baby poop and the best product to get stains out of bibs. Then comes the Tupperware and jewelry party stages and your parents' 25th and grandparents' 50th wedding anniversaries. One of the most significant stages of parenthood is when your children graduate from high school and you have mixed feelings between saying to yourself, "Did I do a good enough job that these kids can really be out on their own?" or are you putting the suitcases out on the front porch and raising a flag the day after graduation?

Then come the weddings. You didn't know that your daughters and your nieces and nephews were old enough to get married. "Did I look that young when I got married?" you say to yourself.

All of a sudden you are a Great Aunt or Heaven forbid a grandmother! I personally found "Grandmother hood" a joy. At first I was only a grandma to the girls' many cats. That got me used to being called "Grandma" long before it really happened! I was 50 years old before I actually became a grandmother so there really wasn't a trauma. My sister already had 6 grandchildren. My friends were having their share already too. *I was ready!*

My first grandchild
Montana Lynn, 1998
Ken Sklute /www.KenSklute.com

I was my daughter's birthing coach and her sister assisted. The three of us were there together to welcome this wonderful little person into the world. Montana was born on Aunt Tracy's birthday, September 11, 1998 and Aunt Tracy was the first person Montana saw when she was born. Tears and Smiles. "Is she really mine?" Tricia asked. This was a beautiful beginning to a new era, new possibilities and for now, it was just the four of us.

Tracy took videos of the whole birthing process. Or at least she *thought* she was taking videos. Tricia wasn't sure she wanted all of this on film, but Tracy really wanted to do it and after all…it *was* her birthday too. So Tricia said she could be the photographer. The doctor had instructed Tracy on where to stand for the most tasteful angles. She was doing everything right and only stopped a few times to gaze at her sister, her new niece and me with amazement at the miracle of what was happening. Fate made the decision for both of them. Tracy had never hit the "record" button and even though the video camera seemed to be filming, absolutely nothing had been recorded!

I told Tracy later, "It was God's plan so that out of the whole world, the three of us would be the only people to experience and remember those moments. Montana's birth was meant to be shared only by us."

As Montana grew up, she couldn't pronounce her "g's" yet, so she called me "Mamaw" instead of "Grandma". She chose my name herself. I have been "Mamaw" ever since to all my grandchildren. Later on I found out that the word "Mamaw" is French for "grandmother". Since then, my lovely daughters and son-in-laws have given me five handsome grandsons and they all call me "Mamaw". Having all of them run to me with wide open arms when they see me yelling "Mamaw!" is my reward for tolerating the teenage years I experienced with my own daughters.

If I had known being a grandma was this much fun, I would have skipped my own daughter's trying teenage years and started here first! It's my second chance to watch *my* children grow up again, only this time, I have so much more experience and let's face it … you really *can* send them home when you're done! Being a grandma is the very best part of life!

Science and a good sense of humor are making me feel better about aging. Overnight creams, wrinkle creams, anti-aging creams, age spot remover, masks, facial hair exfoliaters, cellulite removers, fake hair, fake eyebrows, fake eyelashes, fake boobs, fake butts, tooth whiteners, (for in-the-mouth or out-of-the mouth whiteness!), exercise tapes, fitness gyms, tummy tucks and the Big Mama of them all... *plastic surgery!* I haven't tried that yet, but the possibility hasn't been ruled out.

Appliance manufacturers are making the letters on the appliances bigger and easier to read for us Baby Boomers. Hearing aids are hardly noticeable with modern technology and Lord knows we need them after the outrageously loud music of the 60's ad 70's.

We have graduated bifocals and trifocals and drug store "cheaters" that my friends and I can pass around the table in a restaurant to read our menus! Coloring your hair at home is a breeze and we have a product to temporarily color the roots in between colors. I can run, jump, and ride a horse and hike, if I chose to ...because they have Depends. "No unsightly, embarrassing spots!"

Oh, my God! Just like dad once said, how "did this happen to me?"

As hard as aging is at times, a parent still takes a lot of pride in the accomplishments of the next generation as you watch it grow and even though they could never imagine it...they turn into YOU. There have been extremely difficult stages in my life process too. I don't like to talk about them much but it is necessary to learn from them. Probably the most difficult times were when I had to watch someone I love lose a child. God touched them to give them strength. They touched me.

My grandmother lost *her* child, my dad, and it killed her. She died just three months later of a broken heart.

Hartenfeld Family Album. Photographer, Barbara Hartenfeld circa 1991

She explained, "It's just not right when a child dies before you. It's out of order. It's just not right."

I have seen miracles as well.

Within one month of each other, my grandson, Ryan endured life-saving open-heart surgery and I survived parathyroid surgery. We both got better and were able to add years to our lives together. Ryan, now 7, plays football, soccer, basketball and runs with the best of them. He calls the scar on his chest from the surgery a reminder of the day Jesus gave him a new life.

I have watched friends and families face insurmountable challenges and witness miracles of their own. Some friends lost their battles. Others grew from them. Yet somehow we all go on. I have added one of my favorite verses to close this chapter. I would like to share it with you and hope that you remember it always:

Footprints in the Sand

One night a man had a dream.
He dreamed he was walking along the beach with the Lord.
Across the sky flashed scenes from his life.
For each scene, he noticed two sets of footprints in the sand;
One belonged to him, and the other belonged to the Lord.
When the last scene of his life flashed before him,
He looked back at the footprints in the sand.
He noticed that many times along the path of his life
There was only one set of footprints.
He also noticed that it happened at the very lowest and saddest times in his life.
This really bothered him and he questioned the Lord about it.
"Lord, You said that once I decided to follow You,
You'd walk with me all the way.
But I have noticed that during the most troublesome times in my life
there is only one set of footprints.
I don't understand why, when I needed You most,
You would leave me.
The Lord replied, "My precious child, I love you and would never leave you.
During those times of trial and suffering, when you see only
one set of footprints, it is then that I carried you."

Author Unknown

So you see, my dear daughters, life isn't always what we imagine it should be but it's what we make of it. If you have a situation you cannot change, change the way you think about it. Get to know yourself through your own challenges, trust your instincts and discover the magnificent women you were meant to be. Live life to the fullest and always be true to yourself. Enjoy your journey and always, *always* have a good sense of humor!

I have loved you forever. I hope I have prepared you for what is ahead. If you haven't been listening, imagine me in the great beyond years from now, looking down on you whispering in your ear, *"I told you so!"*

Through all the good times, the bad times, and all those in between-the two of you are the best thing I ever did!

And remember, the next time YOU look into the mirror, like it or not, you may just have grit your teeth and admit to yourselves,

"Mirror, mirror on the wall, I am my Mother after all!"

With a Lifetime of Love,
Your Mom

About the Author

Barbara Leigh Hartenfeld is the mother of two beautiful daughters and grandmother of six and in spite of unexpected surprises that life unpredictably handed her, she has thoroughly enjoyed the ride! Aging is inevitable and although she has fought it all the way, aging has given her wisdom, insight and a sense of humor to give her the audacity to think her experiences just may help the next generation—especially her daughters-to accept the process gracefully.

She has lived in Phoenix, Arizona for twenty years after growing up in Ohio and living in cities all around this great country, dragging her daughters along. Retired from the printing and publishing industry after twenty-five years, she is a Prayer Chaplain at Unity of Phoenix, is a professional seamstress, and an exceptional hands-on grandmother.

Barbara loves life and is always excited to see what's next around the corner and encourages everyone she knows to reach for the brass ring and laugh. Laugh a lot!